MW00985489

Praise for John Dorsey:

"Outlaws in literature are rogues who carry no gun, but fire into the center of our awareness. They use the present, past, and interior world of their dreaming and living. John Dorsey has done a hell of a job! This book will give you a thought provoking introduction to Dorsey's style and talent. I find his writing clear, weirdly funny, moving, and sorrowful. If I were to compare John Dorsey to a respected literary figure, it would have to be Ed Abbey. Both were protectors and observers and laid it out to be remembered!"

-Ann Menebroker, *Author of tiny teeth: The Wormwood Review Poems* (R.L. Crow Publications, 2004).

"I read John Dorsey's compelling, lyrical book in one sitting. He mixes beautiful imagery, insight, candor, vulnerability and wit.What a very cool sandwich! :)"

-ellyn maybe, Author of *the cowardice of amnesia* (2.13.61 Publications, 1998).

More praise for John Dorsey:

"I always know when I am reading a John Dorsey poem. His style is uniquely his. It's as unmistakable as a Greg Corso or a Kell Robertson poem. It's playful, dark, bardic and authentically American."

-Todd Moore, Author of *Dillinger's Thompson* (Phony Lid Publications, 2002).

"I've written about John Dorsey before. He's a vagabon dangel, a word lunatic, a visionary. I saw him read at The Beat Museum and it blew me away. If Gregory Corso and Allen Ginsberg have a spiritual heir, it's John Dorsey. He is carrying the torch,lighting the landscape, singing alone in the wasteland. There is nobody that touches him. Nobody comes close. True genius. Every poem is a complete reward for the moments spent reading it. I feel honored to have met him. I hope to God I see him read again."

-David Barker, Author of *Charles Bukowski Spit in My Face, a Memoir*

Which Way to the River:
New and Selected Poems, 2016-2020

John Dorsey

OSAGE ARTS COMMUNITY

OAC Books
Belle, MO
osageac.org

Acknowledgments

With special thanks to Mark McClane, Tony Hayden, Jason Ryberg & the board members of Osage Arts Community for their continued generous support.

I would like to thank the following publishers & kind friends & supporters.

Maverick Duck Press, Victor Adam Clevenger, Crissy Staton, Rebecca Schumejda, Mike & Eva West, D.R. Wagner, Al Winans, William Taylor Jr., Lois McCure-Smith, Rob Dyer, Mike James, Christopher Harter, David Pratt, Matthew Shaw, Chris Knopp, Erica Johnson, Sam Rikard, Michael Hathaway, Justin Karcher, Jocelyne Desforges, Michael Curran, Wesley Scott McMasters, Pete Faziani, Matthew Quinton Compson, S.A. Griffin, Larry Gawel, Carson Parish, Steve Miller, Charles Joseph, Nathan Stolte, Dianne Bosenik, John Burroughs, Daniel Crocker, Chase Dimock, Gary Cummiskey, David E. Oprava, Steve Goldberg, Chris Lance, Michael Clay, Johnny Olson, John & Dawn Clayton, Kevin Ridgeway, Jonie McIntire, Shelly Fank, Kevin M. Hibshman, Jason Baldiner, James Benger, Kris Collins, Agnes Vojta, Heath Brougher, Jason Shelley, Jeff & Alfier, Marc Burseke, Bradford Middleton, David Yates, Martin Appleby, Cristen Hemingway Jaynes, Tim Tarkelly, Scot D. Young, Michael Behle, Michael Joseph Arcangelini, Pete Donohue, Adrian Manning, Bill Roberts, Bob Branaman, Edwin Sellors, Michelle Storer, Paul Koniecki, Mandy Szostek, Jason Mayer, Ed & Eva Gehlert--Belle Book & Candle, Gerard Malanga, Nolan Stolz, Richard Modiano & the kind staff of the Beyond Baroque Arts Center, Mathew Haines, Dan Wright, Taylor Denise Teachout, Greg Edmondson, Luke Kuzmish, Shawn Pavey, Crazy Mark, John Walz, Raegan Sawyer, Jason Kloock, Laura Martin, Mj Taylor, Brett M. Jurgens, Cherie Bullock, RA Washington, Jennifer Soff, Noah Saar, Jessica Rumbaugh, Bridget Delgado, Brain McGettrick, Scott Wozniak, Damian Rucci, Brett Underwood, Stef Russell, Jim McGowin, My Parents, & so many other people I happen to be forgetting right now because I'm not a good record keeper. I love you.

Table of Contents

Setting a Wasp on Fire / 1

Come Back to the 5 & Dime Crazy Mark
    Crazy Mark / 2

Jason Ryberg Sings an Homage to Bon Jovi / 3

13 Ways of Pan Frying an Armadillo / 4

Poem for Joey Patton / 5

Things You Gave Me / 6

Poem for Brittany / 7

Belle Missouri a Rose by Any Other Name / 8

I Was Told the Revolution Would Not
    Be Televised / 9

Emily Dickinson Died for This / 10

Captain America & Billy / 11

The Biscuit Eater of Penn Hills / 12

Jason Ryberg Says I Write Depressing Poems or
    National News Story 1932 / 14

In Pornography Young Lovers are Timeless / 15

Rodney Watches the News / 16

Gregory in Dannemora / 18

A Yellow Cadillac is a Passport to Solicitation / 19

Pandemic River Poem / 20

Songs About Vaginas / 23

In Bloom / 24

Face to Face With a Lizard / 25

Poem for Lester Madden / 26

Poem for Lester Madden #2 / 27

The War Brides of Wheeling, West Virginia / 28

Stimulus Checks for the Dead / 31

You Don't Have to Go Home
    But You Can't Stay Here / 37

Chase Dimock's Pink Flamingos / 38

A Handful of Dead Beetles / 39

Solitary Confinement / 40

Eating Fried Chicken While Wearing
    a Face Mask / 41

Poem for David Taylor's Girlfriend / 42

On a Train in Charing Cross / 43

I Left My Heart in Massapequa / 44

What My Grandmother Would Say
    About All This / 45

My Aunt Wasn't Billy the Kid / 46

They're Dying in Never Never Land / 49

Poem for Matthew Haines' Imaginary Motorcycle / 50

Retirement Year / 51

Thoughts After Sitting in Daniel Crocker's
    Basement / 52

The End of the World Has Already
    Come and Gone / 53

Poem to the Purple Haired Girl at the
    Belle, Missouri Subway / 54

The Prettiest Girl in the Pandemic / 55

Belle, Missouri, During the Pandemic
    on a Wednesday / 56

Poem for Donald J. Trump / 57

The End of the World is Just the Beginning / 58

Anything With Feathers / 61

You Can't Get Blood From the Dead / 63

Greg Before the Fall of the Berlin Wall / 64

Annette is Always With You / 65

The Prettiest Girl in La Junta, Colorado / 67

The Ballad of Mick Ronson / 68

Crystal / 69

Flashlight Neon Light / 70

Color Theory in the Summer of 1980 / 71

Radio Cities & Number One Records / 73

Wrestling With the Bear / 74

The Finger Has Got to Come Off / 75

Jason Baldinger Talks About the Future / 76

Perpetual Motion / 77

As Curtis Drives By / 80

Greg's Mantra / 81

Detroit Airport en Route to London / 82

Detroit Airport en Route to London #2 / 83

Poem for Damian Rucci / 84

Outlaws in Middle Age / 85

At the Venture Hostel / 86

Beth Saves My Life / 87

A Castle Made of Cigarette Butts / 88

Poem for Winston Trew / 89

Kristen at the Spitfire / 93

Sea Shanty After Gregory Corso / 94

Gregory on Vine Street / 95

Can't Take Me Alive / 99

Poem for Mark Pearce / 100

Proverbs / 101

Poem for Curtis Hayes / 102

Consider Yourself Lucky / 103

Beth From Brixton / 104

Greg & the Spiders From Mars / 105

Picker / 109

Poem for Karen / 111

Having the Croup in 1979 / 115

Poem for Sue / 116

Washington D.C. at the End of the
    Reagan Era / 117

Mr. Wilson Had a Seahorse / 118

In Gym Class / 119

At Sixteen / 120

The Benefits of Cerebral Palsy at Fifteen / 121

Disability in the Age of Disco: The New Hope / 122

Napoleon at Eight Years Old / 123

Every Year at the Children's Hospital / 124

Tim Yost Wore a Sailor Suit / 125

My Brother Could've Been a Monster / 127

How It Goes Now / 128

The Limits of Cerebral Palsy / 129

What Passes for Salvation in Salina, Kansas / 133

Checking the Weather Report at 3 am / 135

The Way of Dandelions / 136

Killing the Wrong Dog / 137

Janna / 138

At Jerry's Restaurant in Weatherford,
    Oklahoma / 139

A Paper Chicken Doesn't Need Wings / 140

Milkshakey / 141

Poem for Nick McClane / 142

Boo Radley Will No Longer Protect Us / 143

Poem for Olin Marshall / 147

A History of Bite Marks / 149

Walking After Midnight in Linn, Missouri / 150

In Front of Magic Mike's / 151

Poem for J.P. / 152

Wolfgang / 154

Caroline Haiku / 155

Coco Malone is a Bad Bitch / 156

Toledo Girls / 158

The End of the Line / 159

Birthday Poems for the Dead / 161

Your Daughter's Country / 162

My Grandmother's Half Sister / 164

Aunt Mary / 165

We Were Still Brave Then / 166

Poem for Mary Anthony / 168

Gasconade Haiku / 169

First Impressions of Belle, Missouri / 170

Tommy / 171

The War at Home / 172

His Summer Place / 173

White Castle on New Year's / 174

Dressing a Deer in Yellow Springs, Ohio / 175

Belle the Musical / 177

Poem for Larry Gawel / 178

What's Left of Love / 179

On Water Street / 180

When Terry was in Rescue Crisis / 181

Me & Bobby Mcgee / 182

Dean / 183

From Memory / 184

Poem for Oscar on a Life Well Lived / 185

River People / 186

Andrew / 187

The Ballad of Emilie Rose / 188

Where the Prom Queen Ends Up or
    Poem for Kristen / 191

Creatures of Our Better Nature / 193

The Goats in December / 194

At Padgett's Place / 195

Huck in Old Age / 196

Another Reason Why I Love This Town / 197

Gasconade Bloodlines / 198

Poem for Donald Lev / 199

Poem for Felino / 200

Questions for Marlon Harris / 201

Wendy Has Never Marched on Selma / 202

Free as a Bird / 203

Anthony Bourdain Crosses the River
    of the Dead / 204

The Ballad of Pegleg & Double Stamp / 205

On or at the Frontier / 206

Poem for Edward Gehlert / 207

Passing Through Leadwood / 208

The Gasconade River is
    a Metaphor for Your Life / 210

A Ghost is an Unforgiving River / 211

On a Lazy Summer Day / 212

Rosalea Ain't Dead Yet / 214

Couch Poem / 217

Getting Lucky / 218

Prostate of the Union / 219

Lean / 220

Bridget / 221

Dying like Dogs / 225

The Postman Never Screams Twice / 227

In Kansas Thinking of You / 229

The Patriotic Gutters of Purcell, Oklahoma / 230

Tammy Talks Tough / 232

Tammy Practices the Art of Negotiation
    in Rolla, Missouri / 234

More Tattoos than Teeth / 239

Sunrise is a Fragile Lover / 240

No Phone Booths / 241

Puberty was a Fever Dream / 242

Old Greg is a Rooster / 243

Scott Wannberg Nearly Broke My Hand
    in a Stockon Denny's / 244

John Berryman Diving School / 245

It's a Wonderful Life, Somewhere / 246

George Bailey Doesn't Live Here / 247

Outlaws & Burned Out Bookstores:
    A Detroit Poem / 248

Fake News, Real Blues / 249

At Popeyez Bar & Restaurant / 253

At Oscar's Classic Diner / 254

At the Glory Hole / 255

J & J's Café on a Sunday Afternoon / 256

Linzi / 257

Moon Over Eufaula, Oklahoma / 261

Poem For Denis Johnson / 262

Diabetes Poem / 263

Poem for Denis Johnson #2 / 264

A Tow Truck Named Desire / 265

Mythology Begins With Fire / 266

On Eva's Birthday / 267

Goat Song / 268

Rocky Mountain Poem / 269

Peter Pan in Carhartts / 270

Spiders the Size of Dogs / 271

Lew Welch Returns From the Woods / 272

Lew Welch Returns From the Woods #2 / 273

Lew Welch Returns From the Woods #3 / 274

Heart / 275

Poem for Todd / 276

Glass City Lolita / 277

At New Derry Theater / 278

The Midwestern Guide to Time Travel / 279

Hey Joe / 280

Godless Animals / 283

In 1954 / 284

Braddock Serenade / 285

What Independence Meant in Irwin,
    Pennsylvania / 286

The Mark Twain Speech / 287

The Boy from Bartlesville / 288

Pigpen / 289

Tough Love / 290

Ray Gene / 291

Ray Gene #2 / 292

Punk Rock at 45 / 293

Cool like Whip / 295

Bugsy Siegel's Desert Rose / 299

The Only Thing / 300

Nikki, in the Summer Heat / 301

Nikki, Full of Grace / 302

Degrees of Gray on Ashland Ave / 303

This Street Feels Like Redemption / 305

Poem for Ray Patrick / 306

Terry at 5150 / 307

Gay Marriage in Second Floor Hallway / 308

The Real World on Collingwood Blvd. / 309

Jeff Walked In / 310

Richard's Heart / 311

The Last Voyage of Captain Black / 312

Heart like a Loaded Gun / 313

High Level Cafe Poem / 314

Nikki, Last Stand at Murphy's / 315

Marlon / 316

The Last Days of the Revolution / 317

Rodney was Afraid / 318

Scott Wannberg as an Old Man / 320

Poem for My Aunt on Her Birthday / 321

Letting the Meat Rest / 323

The Alligator Man / 327

The Prettiest Girl in Moscow, Kansas / 329

Bone Silo / 330

Sunny Side Uprising / 331

Don't Flip the Boat / 332

The Years We Remained Anonymous / 333

The Loons of Walker Lake / 334

A Town With No Roosters / 335

Parker Barrows / 336

For 35 Years / 337

Ladies Night at the Belle Fair / 338

Flight Patterns / 339

County Route 705 / 340

The Colorado Cafe at High Noon / 341

The Dogs / 342

Sadie / 343

Home Cooking / 344

Killing Two Stones with One Heart / 346

The Rabid Dogs of Winter / 348

The Beautiful People / 349

Rodney Says / 351

Poem for My Parents / 352

Cherry Bomb & Boxcar Bertha / 353

The Rainbow Family Would Never Have You / 354

Poem On My 40th Birthday / 356

Dear Phil / 357

The Stigmata of Crazy Mark / 361

The Ghosts of Kell Robertson's Chickens / 362

Everette Maddox Comes to Belle / 363

Song of the Dying Possum / 364

Poem on Brian Felster's 53rd Birthday / 365

Emilie / 366

Chicken Hungry / 367

My First Wife / 368

Looking for Fathers / 370

13 Ways of Looking at a
    Dying Chinese Town / 372

Poem For Kate Marino / 373

Poem For Steven Miller & Brandt Dykstra / 374

Earl / 375

John Prine Never Wrote
   a Song About That / 377

The Gummy Bear Vortex / 378

Pete Seeger Sings to the Moonlight / 379

Future City, Illinois / 380

Frank O'Hara is Dead / 381

Poem for David Greenspan / 382

To Kell / 383

Mozart and Bobby Driscoll / 384

Swallowing A Hornet's Nest / 385

We Are Still The Future / 386

Poem for David Laws / 387

At 59 / 388

Revenge of the Creature / 391

The Bride of Frankenstein Goes Country / 392

House of Wax / 393

The Nosebleed Seats in Heaven / 397

The Hills Have Eyes / 399

The Deer Hunter / 400

The Last Night at Teatro / 402

Making Weight / 403

Being the Fire / 405

Huck's River, Philadelphia / 407

Singh's Song / 408

Philadelphia Gentrification Poem / 410

Children of The Cornbread / 411

Y2K: A Love Story / 412

212 Hours / 413

Channeling Bill Bixby / 414

The Treasure of Sam Ryan / 416

1228 Spruce Street / 417

Sam Ryan Goes to Hollywood / 418

The War on Terror and Baklava / 419

Dog Shit and Moonlight / 420

Ballad of the One Eyed Beast / 421

Indian Summer in December / 422

Appalachian Homage to Cid Corman / 423

20 Miles from Winter's Bone / 424

Poet Laureate of the Dancing Rabbit / 425

Belle, Missouri: A Book of Hours / 426

The Dinner Belle Always Rings Twice / 427

Our Friend in Belle / 428

The Village People of Belle / 429

Gasconade River Song / 430

Gasconade River Song #2 / 431

Gasconade River Song #3 / 432

Gasconade River Song #4 / 433

Gasconade River Song #5 / 434

Gasconade River Song #6 / 435

Gasconade River Song #7 / 436

Gasconade River Song #8 / 437

Gasconade River Song #9 / 438

Gasconade River Song #10 / 439

Coming of Age River / 440

No Women / 441

Detroit Poem / 442

Poem for Greg Peters / 443

Poem for Craig Cody / 444

Eric / 446

Patrice / 448

Pam / 449

Bianca / 450

Brian / 451

Alex / 452

Debbie / 453

Darcie / 454

Glass City Mantra / 455

Jessica Keeps a Rotten Watermelon / 456

Poem for Cherie / 457

Smells like Teen Moms: A Poem
    for the Lucky Club / 458

Poem for Dan O'Neill / 459

At the Model T Casino / 460

Ryberg's Castle / 461

Poem for Trixie / 462

The Russian Sonny and Cher / 463

Poem for Crawdad Nelson / 464

Cow Shit, Texas / 465

Your Last Cerveza / 466

Poem for Kell Robertson / 467

Todd / 468

Irina / 469

The Fight Club House / 470

Ryan / 471

Rock of Love / 472

Happy Hour at the Gold Coin Saloon / 473

Rocky Mountain High / 474

Ed / 475

Tripping at the Olive Garden / 476

Jane Fonda Never Said Hello / 477

The Dean of the Deli / 478

Poem for Jeff Cannon / 479

Round Corner Tavern Poem / 480

Running into Gene Avery in the Park / 481

Scott Wannberg Waves Goodbye
   to Sacramento / 482

Sandy Thomas Goes to Paris / 483

The Ghost of Sacramento Past / 484

Sixty Miles West / 488

Your First Words / 489

The Terrible Twos / 490

Three Candles / 491

Middle Age / 492

Your 5th & 6th Symphony / 493

Swansong / 494

How Did I Get Here?

I've asked myself that very question so many different times in a life I've been so fortunate to get to live. From my beginnings in Greensburg, Pennsylvania to my drunken college years in Philly to years spent starving, not eating for 3 or 4 days in a clip in Toledo, Ohio, where I met friends who still make my heart swell with love, to these more recent times in Wisconsin and in Belle, all the while getting to travel around the world writing poems, screenplays, newspaper articles, seeing my work published, filmed, recorded, and archived, something I'd always dreamt of, but never thought would actually happen.

All of this brings me to this most recent work, all completed during my time in Osage Arts Community, with the exception of a few pieces created at Paul ArtSpace in St. Louis, which I found rather randomly in my quest for another residency after my time at the Collingwood Arts Center came to a close sooner than I would've liked.

The poems in this book are portraits of people and places that have all been a part of my life at one point or another, but they're all Missouri poems, at least in the sense that they were all written here. They pick up where my reader Appalachian Frankenstein left off in 2015. I chose to put them all together right now because I find myself at a crossroads in my creativity, looking for a new direction, much like I was when I first came to Missouri from the frosty winters of Wisconsin. I've also had certain health issues that have lent this whole process a certain sense of added urgency that comes with middle age. My hope is that these two larger collections are just the beginning and that in time I can put everything together in one huge opus that nobody will even be able to bind, but this is just one step in the process that needed to happen.

I'm a different writer than when many of these poems were first written, hopefully a little smarter, definitely a bit older, good or bad, there's no stopping time. There are poems in this book that will offend certain people, but that's okay, there are also poems that will make them laugh, frown and maybe shed a few tears, but they're all as honest as I can make them. I'm just glad I got the chance to write them. Often these feel like dark days, and I'll admit that I need to keep making new work and putting it out there just to remind myself that I'm a living, breathing, being, still capable of translating memory and bringing a bit of light into the world. These poems are hope, so just enjoy them.

-John Dorsey, Belle, Missouri, 9-1-20.

for Victor Adam Clevenger
& Rebecca Schumejda

New & Uncollected Poems

Setting a Wasp on Fire

for jason ryberg

i think about it
how the roman dead loved their children once
how we're not special
how flesh burns
just as well in any century

as i aim a grill lighter
straight at the heart of a red carpenter wasp
as crazed drivers venture down the county route
to get their medicine

my grandmother would've said
that bee could be the ghost of george floyd
just looking for a torch

so be gentle with death
it is more than just the anniversary
of our bones.

Come Back to the 5 & Dime Crazy Mark
Crazy Mark

i imagine your youth
not as some dust bowl
of right wing political commentary
with good looking people
who can always afford
to get their prescriptions filled

but as a true swamp of innocence

we both live in a country
where history walks with a limp

nobody goes around nursing a bad cough
for the sake of mystery

so when i call to you in the street
just know
that i mean it.

Jason Ryberg Sings an Homage to Bon Jovi

like a glass of water
you are the child of a river

just remember the words
that brought you here
& move on.

GLASS OF WATER
BORN OF RIVER, SEA,
PRIMORDIAL FLUID

13 Ways of Pan Frying an Armadillo

crazy mark says you'll need a good skillet
& the right amount of spices

also it's better if the moon is full
& rain is tapping against
your kitchen window just so

after all we're not savages here

but anything tastes better with hot sauce
that's just a fact

if the poor creature struggled
before finding true love
& dying peacefully in the tall grass
that just adds to the flavor

when i mention the risk of leprosy
he says you can fry
almost anything out
even the scent of death
blowing in the missouri wind.

Poem for Joey Patton

joey we hadn't eaten all day
walking around venice in the rain
in search of a meatball sandwich

you were the only thing
that made me laugh

beat had nothing to do with it
brother
you were human.

Things You Gave Me

for my grandmother

a healthy distrust of doctors
& the law

hay fever
short stumps for legs
a sense of humor

an ear for good gossip

a taste for fast food
& anything
that wasn't made
by your own hands.

Poem for Brittany

i have seen you on the streets of new orleans
taking photos with well meaning tourists
for half finished beers on bourbon st
crossing venice blvd wearing blue socks
in a shroud of rain
chasing moloch
in a famous blue raincoat
shouting moloch
praying to moloch
that when morning comes
your shadow will recognize your smile
& that my heavy heart
full of forgotten cities
will be able
to carry the weight
of your love.
on its shoulders.

Belle Missouri a Rose by Any Other Name

the klu klux klan drops off pamphlets
at our local bookstore
& nobody says anything

& people are dying in the streets for nothing
dying in their homes for nothing

when there are flowers
planted right outside my house
& it's their color
that makes them beautiful.

I Was Told the Revolution Would Not Be Televised

but everything is

blood just looks better
on a big screen.

Emily Dickinson Died for This

the sound of rain
in the missouri sky
social distancing
from hummingbirds.

Captain America & Billy

at fourteen my brother was obsessed with easy rider
& the soft purr of a rickenbacker bass

hog heaven was the scent of gasoline & perfume
& the roar of engines on a small screen

we'd drink mad dog 20/20 out of paper bags
under the old movie theater sign
with its letters dangling
like a long forgotten ransom note

he was captain america
i was billy
& george hanson rolled into one
& steppenwolf was still the birdsong
of modern myth

& before i maxed out my credit cards
we'd eat huge dinners in a strip mall t.g.i. friday's
& fill ourselves with red wine
in the middle of the afternoon
imagining we were in the french quarter
or at least a few counties over
not wanting to think about
the coming pennsylvania winter
or that we might never end up
going anywhere at all.

The Biscuit Eater of Penn Hills

when my brother was 3 or 4
he'd steal dog biscuits
from under our grandmother's
kitchen counter

& when those milk-bone boxes ran dry
from the dogs themselves
with their brittle bones
hardly able to put up a fight
against his white baby teeth & shiny coat

he would just crunch away in a dark corner
hoping for enough time
to lap up every loose crumb

sometimes he got lucky
others my mother would snatch them
a soggy half-eaten boneyard
from his hot little fingers

& he would sit there wailing
tears rolling down his cheeks

his first demons

his could feel them in his bones
wagging their tails
& nipping at his heels
from darker corners.

Jason Ryberg Says I Write Depressing Poems or National News Story 1932

if i'd written about the lindbergh baby
the kidnappers would've probably just
slit its throat from the get go

& not even bothered with the ransom.

In Pornography Young Lovers are Timeless

kissing like wolves
whose lips are code for nothing.

Rodney Watches the News

the last time it meant anything
was right before
the space shuttle challenger exploded
taking all of his childhood with it

when an unmowed lawn
might have meant a black eye
if this wasn't a snow day

his mother yelling in the yard
for his father to stop
beating the dog
in front of the children

some seasons never change

now the political climate just means
thinking about the snow chains
he'll need to put on his truck

but that's not news

blood is still stick thicker
than water here

it is a family tradition

stronger than the roots of trees
like the bees that come back in summer
it stings everything it touches.

Gregory in Dannemora

you were not shelley's rose colored skin
but byron's dirty fingernails

myth burying genius
in its sunday clothes

uninvited you drank in

every word

you could swallow.

A Yellow Cadillac is a Passport to Solicitation
for s.a. griffin

in toledo we listened to neil young
outside a bar where a prostitute
had chased us into the street

in west virginia we drove past storefront windows
that harbored hate groups
in search of chilli dogs

in the ohio river valley
you stole some fucked up ceramic dinnerware
from behind a dumpster

where they have been
guarding the dead
for generations.

Pandemic River Poem

here even the babies are ugly
when you look at their reflection
in the water.

Fort Pitt Tunnel Blues
(Maverick Duck Press, 2020)

Songs About Vaginas

at 37 my brother struts like ted nugent
in our parents' basement
just like he did
back in high school

it's like he's trapped in a time machine
shaped like a muscle car full of regrets

the women he sings about
have never been real

they've never shopped for groceries
or fumbled around for loose change
on the pennsylvania turnpike
only to have it all
lead to nowhere.

In Bloom

it isn't just a nirvana song
or pair of headphones
dragging you into the past

it's a street corner
where a girl in a cast
sells $5 roses
on a warm day
in pittsburgh

with a smile that says
your dream or mine.

Face to Face With a Lizard

for christian clevenger

milkman i wouldn't worry too much
about the lizards in the couch in my garage

just think about your future prom date
wiggling all over your body

close your eyes
turn off the lights

& call it young love.

Poem for Lester Madden

even the dead can see the lights from the highway
i imagine you were an olympic swimmer

that you once kissed a girl from zelienople
on a first date at baldinger's
who had sugar sweet lips

you were a lucky guy
that's further
than i've ever gotten.

Poem for Lester Madden #2

sometimes a shark attack is an act of love.

The War Brides of Wheeling, West Virginia

their letters have been lost to time
in a discarded mailbox
full of cobwebs

outside of the only gas station in town

this isn't how it was supposed to go
their love was never meant
to fade away.

Stimulus Checks for the Dead
(River Dog, 2020)

Stimulus Checks for the Dead

I.

more than a million ghosts
will eat better than you tonight

sleeping along the borders of history

of moon landings

of great speeches of empathy

not tear gas

not children in cages

not batons across the neck
of a river.

II.

the dead don't need our help

the dead never wear face masks

the dead keep everything off the books

the dead bump into each other in the clouds

the dead give eskimo kisses to the dead

the dead are a pile of worry

the dead are a mountain of regrets

the dead are a great poem

the dead are a bad poem

the dead are a beautiful girl who will never grow old

the dead are a warm foxhole

the dead are a great love story

the dead are your mother's broken heart

the dead are your father's missed opportunities

the dead are a friend that you couldn't save from the dead

the dead went to your high school

the dead puked in your car

the dead lost their virginity to the dead

the dead died of cancer

the dead died of heart attacks

the dead died of aids

the dead died because of their skin color

the dead died for the right to love anyone they want

the dead died of hunger

the dead died of loneliness

the dead were murdered by the dead

the dead hummed gershwin in concentration camps

the dead loved you with all their hearts

the dead sometimes said things
they didn't mean.

Violence is Golden
(Analog Submission Press, 2020)

You Don't Have to Go Home
But You Can't Stay Here

for chris knopp

true love is six feet away
from where i am standing

the moon is a beautiful sinking boat
when it winks at toledo

my heart can't whistle

the bar is closed

the sky is a dead industry

the only songs i know

are about girls.

Chase Dimock's Pink Flamingos

do the birds call to you
as you cross ventura blvd
for indian food
and late '70s game shows

or is it your voice
that sings in the shower
thinking about the next lonely boy
like a praying mantis
gliding up your steps.

A Handful of Dead Beetles

won't help you remember
what day it is

only the season
when your grandmother's roses
would spring up every year
& never fail
to prick
your chubby fingers.

Solitary Confinement

my dad always hated
that i never wanted
to go outside

so when i was grounded
he'd make me
put down my books
& go sit under the sun

in a universe so large & lonely
where i was the last surviving
castaway on gilligan's island

transplanted to the front lawn
of a trailer park in pennsylvania

where i listened for the sound of birds

where i didn't dare make a move
on my own.

Eating Fried Chicken While Wearing
a Face Mask

for victor clevenger

it's impossible

i'm just trying to collect
enough wings

to fly away.

Poem for David Taylor's Girlfriend

asking me for $5
because you're cute
just seems weird

we're both ugly on the inside

but at least
i've lived
long enough
to know it.

On a Train in Charing Cross

a teacher gave me a pin
that said translating poetry
is the opposite of war

but i know better
than to ask the dead
for miracles

water is thicker than blood

when you're just trying
to get out
of the rain.

I Left My Heart in Massapequa

for charles purpura

we're all buried
our hearts are inside out

bones have replaced bricks

you always taught me
how to find the humor
in anything

& right now
i just wish
you were here
to rewrite history

& arm wrestle death.

What My Grandmother Would Say About All This

she would eat white castle hamburgers
in abandoned parking lots

& tell me that dead butterflies
have dirty fingers.

My Aunt Wasn't Billy the Kid

after they accused her
of robbing a department store
she never tried to run anywhere

she lost her job
lost her car
lost a sense
of what her future
was even supposed to be

& history
never came looking
to write her story down.

The End of the World is Just the Beginning
(Roaring Junior Press, 2020)

They're Dying in Never Never Land

the unclaimed bodies in potter's field
answer to bobby driscoll now
they will not stay silent
in this generation
of lost boys

this isn't just the song of the south
but everywhere we look

they refuse to do the dance
for peter pan's invisible bones

death doesn't tell the whole story

forget the bodies
they were lives first

laughter & soft hands
feet planted firmly
in the earth.

Poem for Matthew Haines' Imaginary Motorcycle

i for one am glad
your wheels are made of wind

birds can carry blood only so far
before each generation
plants its song
in the soil

as you buzz by it

with all of the passion of the dead
rain slicked with invisible speed.

Retirement Year

my father can't hear anything
so death can sing
as loud as it wants

love has always
kept its distance

the lines in his skin
are an ocean
of memories.

Thoughts After Sitting in Daniel Crocker's Basement

i have never been a first responder
a canary in a coalmine

i have always sung too loudly
in times that demanded silence

made off-color jokes
to shield a cough
from being anything more serious

but now i worry about my father
at war with age
& his own failing ears

his heart once lived
in a wiser country

now it only beats
when it feels like it

i worry about everything
my mother puts in god's hands

suddenly it all feels like
one too many bags of groceries
to take into the house.

The End of the World Has Already Come and Gone

crazy mark tells me
that he was just at a bbq
with twenty other people

& it doesn't matter anyway

there isn't enough sanitizer in the world
to wash the blood
from our hands.

Poem to the Purple Haired Girl at the Belle, Missouri Subway

here you are risking your life
for sandwiches

& so am i

it must be fate.

The Prettiest Girl in the Pandemic

wears a mask
to cover her heart.

Belle, Missouri, During the Pandemic on a Wednesday

here nothing has changed
everyone thinks we're overreacting
angry parents talk about the prom
& missed school trips

young lovers have always died for pageantry

but the truth is
kids will still make babies
in the back of parked cars without
all of the ceremony

the news is a reminder that
the atomic bomb didn't exist
until we built it.

someone says
if we can survive that
we'll certainly
get through this

with or without toilet paper.

Poem for Donald J. Trump

there are no small death rates
only small presidents.

The End of the World is Just the Beginning

i still need water
candy & good memories

i'm still lonely
on a friday night.

The NU Profit$ of P/O/E/T/I/C DI$CHORD,
The Ghosts of Our Words Will Be Heroes in Hell
(OAC Books, 2020)

Anything With Feathers

my grandfather taught me
how to shoot at empty beer cans
how to laugh
when things got tough

he hated banks
& doctors

loved chocolate covered cherries
chipped ham & potato chips on sundays

when they chopped off his legs
he started making hook rugs
with ducks in every pattern
until his vision went

even then
sometimes he would close his eyes
real tight

& flap his arms

up & down

up & down

he was donald duck

he was charles lindbergh

he slept with one eye open
in a hospital bed
in the middle of his living room

he squeezed my hand
& told me not to work too hard
it wasn't worth it

he said anything with feathers
could fly.

You Can't Get Blood From the Dead

for mike james

the sun no longer touches their lips
whatever they knew about love
will remain a mystery.

Greg Before the Fall of the Berlin Wall

in 1984 greg made flowers out of iron & wood
& black ink

molded drama with his bare hands
from clay and the ancient stars
hidden in the city sky

when he drank too much
he could still remember all of the lyrics
to rock you like a hurricane

he could build a trojan horse
for helen of troy
inside his own heart
& tell time by the sun

to keep him
from getting lost.

Annette is Always With You

crazy mark keeps 2 pounds of marijuana
in pringles cans in the cabinet
under his coffeemaker

he keeps his girlfriend on the phone
the entire time he tosses ziplock bags
in my direction

he talks about how her kidneys
failed last week
as if she can't hear him

stopping to cough
while she talks about
which strain helps
with what ails her

they've known each other
since they were kids

he holds the phone tight
against his chest

she's like a patch of daisies
in the florida swamp

if she were to go
the loss would be deeper
than any old can
could fill.

The Prettiest Girl in La Junta, Colorado

works the graveyard shift at the loaf n jug
on the corner of north third street
where the county sheriff
comes to get his coffee
every sunday at 2:32 am

she may be the only girl for miles

he tells her a corny joke
& thinks about what
their children might look like

even though she went to school
with his daughter

while she thinks about pricing toilet paper
& off brand soda
& candy bars covered in sugar
or nothing at all
at this time of night

barely out of high school
it still feels like
she hasn't smiled for a generation

hasn't given her heart
to the wind.

The Ballad of Mick Ronson

for maybe the thousandth time
greg mentions that his father
once compared mick ronson to chet baker

one man's rhythm is never the same as another

there isn't enough whiskey here
to keep his sadness out

it's just a good thing they're both dead
or they'd have to sit here
listening to his story too.

Crystal

at 26
you've already been married
to a neo nazi
engaged to an aging hipster
glued to the couch
with taco bell & mom jeans

you say you're into old school punk
rattling off bands i've never heard of
carrying the weight of the world
in every step

you complain about how
it's too cold to stand outside
to smoke a cigarette

you don't need to look at the moonlight
to blame the sky
for everything.

Flashlight Neon Light

greg smiles as he talks about how his daughter
used to run around the house naked as a baby
singing flashlight neon light

all he needs now
is for her to help him
find the funk

but she won't even answer
his calls anymore

flashlight
neon light
red light

it all comes out like a nursery rhyme
reaching back into the past

the night is young
& all he needs
is to find the funk

he's gotta have that funk

that once sang
all the way
into his heart.

Color Theory in the Summer of 1980

on the news all they talked about
was the hostage crisis
ronald reagan looked like john wayne
with whiter teeth or the ghost of gig young
coming back to bring our boys home
from the past

i drank donald duck grapefruit juice
& made war with plastic army men
on our green shag carpet almost every night
until the sun went down

we always freed the hostages
we always waved the flag
unless i got sleepy

like one night
when i spilled juice
all over the tv

red
white
&
blue

suddenly became blue & green bars
on every channel

my father refused to replace it
for at least 10 years

it was perfectly good

by then the hostages really were free
& my men were buried in the backyard
or taken away in garbage bags

the summer sun was sticky
& blood was the color
it was always
supposed to be.

Radio Cities & Number One Records

greg talks about how his friend richard
once shared the stage with alex chilton

mumbling something about the price
that comes with genius

there were no small notes
in the air
that night

only big stars.

Wrestling With the Bear

for jason baldinger

it's all a circus babe
winter in pittsburgh
is no joke

the bear will show its teeth
whenever it pleases

just watch out for the high wire
& remember that fried chicken
is even better cold.

The Finger Has Got to Come Off

crazy mark crushes his finger
in the back of a dump truck

instead of going to the hospital
he examines the bone

each angle
like the rings on a tree

each crack
a ridge of undiscovered country

clues to a past
that even he can't quite recall

weeks go by
and the skin
just won't heal

he says he'll have to
cut the meat off himself
before it starts to stink
like a dying animal
left to rot
in the woods.

Jason Baldinger Talks About the Future

he says it's all dick pics & robots
from here on out.

Perpetual Motion

in the 1980s
everything was smooth sailing
except
drugs
aids
starvation
exploding space shuttles
&
the threat of foreign wars

we had miami vice
& a small hole
peeking through the ozone layer
from all of those cans of hairspray

everyone in the trailer park
had a waterbed

our neighbors at the top of the hill
got their kids a chihuahua puppy for christmas

they would take turns tossing it
onto the bed

watching the poor thing
sway back & forth
like a drunken sailor

only a few weeks
after bringing it home
it slid right off the bed

snapping its neck
without even a whimper

rubber ball still firmly in its mouth

as a child's birthday party went on
in full swing in the next room

it was so quiet
that we thought
it was playing a game

& then the youngest neighbor boy
started wailing

as his brother approached the body
with plastic army men
as if it was just some peaceful beast
he had killed in battle

their father covered it up
with a beach towel
as their mother asked us
who wanted cake

& somehow like magic
the decade was over
before it had even really
gotten started.

As Curtis Drives By

crazy mark talks about this woman over in byron
who paid him $100 just to lick her asshole

this morning he was knee deep
in chicken shit
looking for eggs
to get through the winter

but she was too crazy
even for him.

Greg's Mantra

down here bowie & prince are like gods
& if you drink enough cheap bourbon
the stars that light the night sky

will always lead you home

even in a dented minivan.

Detroit Airport en Route to London

12 hours sitting in a plastic chair
across from a p.f. chang's
will turn anyone into a prisoner of war.

Detroit Airport en Route to London #2

the security guards look at you
like you want to be there

as you look out longingly
at the last beautiful girl
you may ever see
eating french fries
out of a suitcase.

Poem for Damian Rucci

wanted men are rare
the rest of us
are everywhere.

Outlaws in Middle Age

for david e. oprava

dave & i drink
some indian beer
& fall asleep
before 6 pm

each one dreaming
of women

we'll never get.

At the Venture Hostel

there is a condom machine
in the bathroom

unable to sleep
in the middle bunk

i sit in a shower stall
where babies have probably
been conceived
or left for dead

like all bad decisions

waiting for this night
to disappear.

Beth Saves My Life

for jason shelley

at least four times in thirty minutes
a cab driver from morocco
drops me off
at a reading

that feels like an a.a. meeting

a former revolutionary
walks home alone
in the rain

to feed his cats.

A Castle Made of Cigarette Butts

for bradford middleton

is still a castle
a throne on fire
can still offer
its share of wisdom.

Poem for Winston Trew

you pulled your punches
like a man

& left your blood
on the pavement

so others
could find peace.

Dog Park 2
(River Dog, 2020)

Kristen at the Spitfire

diabetic at 28
after too many
all night ragers
sitting on a corner stool
where you take out your teeth
& place them on the bar

the real ones knocked out
by a guy whose name
you can't even remember

it takes me selling seventeen books
to cover your bar tab
& still you go in for one more
dropping your poems in the snow
leaving them to fly away
to create stories of their own
as you smoke a cigarette
& worry about their future

you hand the bartender your teeth
as collateral

he pours you a boilermaker
figuring whether you come back or not
it's a good way
to get you
to stop talking.

Sea Shanty After Gregory Corso

the sea no longer eats your mother's flesh
but spits her salty reflection back out into the ocean
netting songs to fill the bellies of the dead
where your infant cry is a quiet wave
on church steps

in the morning
the sun will find you dancing
like a seasick sailor

surely
it will.

Gregory on Vine Street

i spend all afternoon searching for you
sleeping if off on a park bench
where you hand me half a warm beer
& a mess of wrinkled poems
scattered like a rat's nest
in a busted suitcase

i should be doing anything
other than this

finding young love and losing it

like a roman candle

like a roller coaster
by the sea
in my heart

like magic

just like that
you're gone

before i can even
finish my beer.

I Bet You Think This Song is About You
(Punk Provincial Press, 2019)

Can't Take Me Alive

drunk on cheap whiskey
greg sits listening
to steely dan again

as if every note is the history
of his life

when i mention that they had to crack open
an old friend's chest the night before
he brushes me off
& talks about his ex-girlfriend

who like an erratic heartbeat
is never coming back.

Poem for Mark Pearce

you tell me about your father
dead at 49

we are all just trying
to keep moving

our hearts under attack
every minute of every day

love isn't a speeding train
but more of a ceasefire
set to music.

Proverbs

three chinese boys
under a tarp in a pickup truck
in the desert
aren't bad hombres

they're just boys

you can't throw
fortune cookie wisdom
at the dead

a quiet rain
will say anything it pleases
to a hawk
on its deathbed

the song inside a pebble
was once a rock.

Poem for Curtis Hayes

you say that everything we can see here
was once a strawberry field
& talk about a girl
who once had a baby in the bathroom
that now has a busted sink
as we sit beside your empty swimming pool
sipping gin & tonics in the sun

the past is a young man's game
its bones good & strong

runaway birds in our infancy
we all make strange sounds
that pass for stories

before we fly away.

Consider Yourself Lucky

for greg

you've sold more paintings
than van gogh

& have two good ears
that can hear regret coming
from a mile away.

Beth From Brixton

i imagine your legs
are paler than the moon
on that long walk home.

Greg & the Spiders From Mars

sitting in his near empty studio
greg says that this feels like
the day david bowie died

but this is nothing like that at all
the walls closing in with silence

for all of the songs
he never took the time
to listen to.

Head On
(Rusty Truck Press, 2019)

Picker

that's what they called him
a finger buried deep in his nose
as a way to cope
with a flabby stomach
& a face covered with so much acne
that it was about as baby soft
as the surface of mars

that was before everyone had anxiety
when ptsd was reserved for people with real problems
when kids threw lit matches at anyone
they couldn't just burn at the stake
when we ate pop rocks & pepsi
because we wanted to spontaneously combust
as if daring god to give it his best shot

his sister sat in the back of the bus
hiding from her own bloodline
denying his existence
to sit next to cheerleaders
who would shoot spitballs
into her greasy black hair
when she wasn't looking

she would just laugh
as if she was in on the joke
saving her tears for after supper

when she could write it all down
in a secondhand trapper keeper
with a wrinkled picture
of mary lou retton
taped to the front

they used to jump rope
in their front yard
with these same kids

their mother used to tell them
they could be whatever they wanted

but she never had to carry
their books in the snow
heavy with the weight of hours

when silence greeted them
in crowded halls

& blood seemed thicker
than almost anything.

Poem for Karen

you mention something
about the quantum physics
of failed love stories

how your heart
is a fortune cookie
split into 68 uneven parts

a stubborn song
that just won't do anything
for its own good

a magnet for numbers
that never work

a sea shanty
for the dead

a dream broken up
& pushed apart
at the seams

you would put tin foil
on the feet of god
if you thought nobody
was looking.

Sick
(Luchador Press, 2019)

Having the Croup in 1979

meant that i couldn't yell
not even on the inside
only whoop like a bird
with my underdeveloped lungs
trying to escape
the trailer park even then
as the knack sang
on the radio
about things
more precious
than air.

Poem for Sue

for a few short hours every week
you helped me forget
about the plastic leg brace
that i had to squeeze
into my right shoe
every morning

helped me work muscles
i've let turn to fat
in middle age
the year i turned thirteen
i ran into you
at a pizza parlor
on my birthday
when you told me
you had cancer

it's your laughter
i hold onto now

good therapy
when i need it most.

Washington D.C. at the End of the Reagan Era

my mother had to fight for me
to able to go on a school trip
where they said
i just wouldn't be able to keep up

they were right

out of breath
i stopped to cry
& run my fingers
across the names
of dead boys
who lost their lives
just trying to keep up.

Mr. Wilson Had a Seahorse

on the corner of his desk
he told me i walked like a duck
flapping his wings
in front of the class
to illustrate his point

he made my friend mark piss himself
instead of letting him go to the bathroom
after he started to cry

even after his father died
mark refused to tear up
because he didn't want anything
running down his face
that reminded him
of saltwater.

In Gym Class

there was always one guy
slower than me

some poor guy with palsy
worse than mine

whose spine curved
like a frightened turtle
at the sight
of a sweaty wrestling mat

thank god for him.

At Sixteen

it seemed like everyone
drove a car but me

as kris & i walked
to the bowling alley
on my birthday

i wrote stories on my arm
in dull ink
faded by the sun

my muscles
weak
swerving
out of control

we were all just looking
for a way to escape

that long walk
home.

The Benefits of Cerebral Palsy at Fifteen

if i had any dexterity
in my right hand at all
i would've tried
to cut my wrists.

Disability in the Age of Disco: The New Hope

in 1977 they kept me in a heated machine
meant for a creature the size of a baby bird
i weighed just over three pounds
& cried through the night

a few weeks out of the hospital
my parents took me
to the drive in
to see star wars
as palm trees swayed
above my head

they were young
& just happy
that i was alive
& everything else
seemed liked a galaxy
far far away.

Napoleon at Eight Years Old

while other boys
ran after lost baseballs
& stolen kisses

i thought
there had to be
more
to life
than this.

Every Year at the Children's Hospital

i'd be filled with dread
having to spend all day
in a waiting room
with other disabled kids
just so a doctor could test my reflexes
& ask me about my day
on an uncomfortable metal table

after more than forty years
it hasn't gotten any better
i still break out in hives
at the thought of having to find parking
in downtown pittsburgh
just thinking about the garage
that my dad would always
have to remember
to bring enough change for

i'm not an animal
tables were made for dinner
& polite conversation
not for sitting on
no matter how great
your day was.

Tim Yost Wore a Sailor Suit

& had physical therapy
in the same room as me

he was so fat
that when they threw a ball at him
it would just bounce off his stomach

he would just giggle
jollier than santa claus
at the first sight
of a snowflake in winter

he'd talk about fishing trips
he'd never get to go on
his father always said one day

i'd struggle to understand him
he came into this world
a few months early
just like me

we were all shoved into a single room
no matter what your issue was
on fridays they made popcorn
salted & placed into brown paper bags
& we watched the same movie
on a reel to reel projector
almost every single week

the hero wasn't like any of us
he could go fishing anytime he wanted
& could swing words
always easy to understand
like a sword
on his tongue.

My Brother Could've Been a Monster

he could've tortured me
for not being able to dance
or walk a straight line
to save my life

instead he was silent

he's silent still
playing music
& smoking weed in the garage
reading a weathered book
about the war of the roses

& there's so much
i'd like to say
to him now.

How It Goes Now

the other day i fell & landed on my back
smacking my head on the cement

i already take enough ibuprofen
to kill a horse

the government says
i'm not disabled enough
to collect a check

that's alright

we all misjudge our steps sometimes
we've all woken up shaking
in the middle of the night.

The Limits of Cerebral Palsy

i can't take a woman from behind
my balance is off
& we'll both roll off
the side of the bed
unsatisfied.

Flycatcher in the Rye
(Analog Submission Press, 2019)

What Passes for Salvation in Salina, Kansas

you cannot buy beer here after midnight
but we watch as a strung out girl
in camouflage yoga pants ties one off
in a gas station parking lot near iron ave

history just moves slower here
with its tall waitresses & buckwheat pancakes
just looking for a little laughter

it's poetry in motion
waiting for the punchline
on handwritten checks
from the local diner

the billboard in the center of town
says that you can have a hysterectomy your way

that's what drives tourism now
removing parts of a whole

with lingering doubts
on our tired tongues

silence is the only form of currency
that the wind seems to recognize

we just accept its terms
& go inside

we are all alone at the party
no matter what time it is

tomorrow all of this
will be someone else's problem.

Checking the Weather Report at 3 am

we measure our moods
by how deep the river is

that isn't passion

young lovers don't drive their cars
to the banks here
like they used to
in 1953

the moonlight doesn't run its fingers
under your grandmother's dress
tapping a flashlight
against the driver's side window
of a steam filled buick

there are rocks here
that we'll never declare
sticks beavers will never build into dams
ghosts that will never die
for our sins.

The Way of Dandelions
for Ron Kolm

everything is wild here
heavy rain & children
who grow like weeds

the sun on your back

you don't even have to like it

it's almost better if you don't.

Killing the Wrong Dog

leaves scatter in the treeline
& mix with your blood

if you shoot your soul
like a disobedient dog
on a warm spring day
you'll need to find
another god
to pray to.

Janna

greg talks about his
ex-girlfriend's multiple personalities

he says that makes
at least two more people
who hate his guts.

- FURTHER
- JACKIE'S DAUGHTERS (lecmo)
- IMAGINARY AUTHORS
- FOR STRANGE WOMEN (lecmo)
- NA NIN
- AUSTIN PRESS

PERFUMES

At Jerry's Restaurant in Weatherford, Oklahoma

a cardboard sign used to proclaim
that blake mcintyre of thomas oklahoma
ate 20 pancakes here

but i stole it right off the wall
& took all of his glory with it
right in the middle of broad daylight

blake you beautiful bastard
there is no more glory in syrup
than there is in blood

you ate 20 pancakes
in the middle of winter
& nobody died
birds didn't sing

the heavens refused to open up.

A Paper Chicken Doesn't Need Wings

to sweat through the night
the clock at the bank on the corner
says it's 89 degrees
in carrollton missouri
just before midnight

history's weather vane
always seems to land on the poor
& the pallets in farmers' fields
always look like bones
at the same time
every morning

blood in
blood out

whole families migrate with the soil

water against our houses
seashells pressed against the ears
of dying men

ghosts of a prior season
have come here
to dream of valor

the wind has no say in any of this
& neither do we.

Milkshakey

i've heard that in kansas
waitresses bring you milkshakes
24 hours a day

that even after the bars close down
you can still get drunk on longing
& possibility

but it's only a dream
like your legs wrapped around me
like a spider in a gunfight
the morning after
we've all gone home.

Poem for Nick McClane

the path of totality
is a girl
just in from the river
making love to you
in a stranger's bathroom
as her parents sit
in the sun
on a wooden deck
holding her baby
on one knee

beautiful things often
eclipse the hands that made them

days like this
are only as hot
as passion will let them be
& no more.

Boo Radley Will No Longer Protect Us

from our own nature
while the blood moon of alabama
hangs around our hearts
like a noose around dreams
in a mute sky
of disbelief

it's all backward here
but none of it
is fiction

young girls let out silent screams
like torch singers
in the alleys of the dead
without even knowing
how they got there

the landscape is a broken time machine
in museums of youthful abandon
dedicated to their grandmother's concerns
as if they never went away

harper lee where are you now

scout finch was once
a feminine flower
of a girl

now she's just a pile of bones

eventually all our role models turn to dust
when what they fight for
are nothing more than words
on a page.

Your Daughter's Country
(Blue Horse Press, 2019)

Poem for Olin Marshall

all my grandmother's cousin ever wanted
was his own pizza & a used lawn tractor
the son of sharecroppers & war heroes
he drove a school bus & raised wild dogs
that bit the hand that fed them
he sat outside by the fire
talking about his dead sister
as if she were a saint

she had been gone since 1973
the same year his wife passed
& he still had never seen a ghost
quite as lovely

his younger brother had been a race car driver
just before the second world war
when he crashed & burned
he left him a small fortune
that was still sitting in the bank
nearly half a century later

on his birthday we convinced him
to get the tractor
but the pizza still felt
like an extravagance

he would just gaze out at his property
in front of the old family general store
spitting dried up chewing tobacco
into a rusted coffee can
harvesting sunlight
without lifting a finger
gathering his history up like dead leaves
like a pile of bones

if the wind had any sense of mercy
it would've taken him too.

A History of Bite Marks

olin's dog bruno
would bite anything
that came near him

when a bat soared past my aunt's ear
as she tried to get some sleep
in the bed of my grandfather's truck
he leaped toward it
like he was chasing a firefly
in the cold west virginia evening

when my grandmother got a new dog
olin offered my cousin amanda & i
2 bucks to wash them both off
in the creek up the way
that was full of cow shit

he nearly tore the poor thing's ear clean off
as they wrestled in the dirty water

he tried to take chunks out of our ankles
if we tried to bathe outside
or sit by the fire
or breathe overly loudly
for any prolonged period
of time.

Walking After Midnight in Linn, Missouri

for jeanette powers

it's the middle of the afternoon
& the jukebox that once offered
a youthful kiss from patsy cline in the moonlight
is now drowned out by the bartender
talking about how the fry cook
is not her boyfriend

sleepy eyed construction workers
are left to dream about true love
on their own as they wander back out
into the cold

their regrets will haunt them
long after the grease
from the fried chicken special
has settled in their stomachs

settling is just the way of things
nobody is searching for anyone
after midnight here

pride only makes you lonely

while the rest of the world
is fast asleep.

In Front of Magic Mike's

we watch from the window
as a drunk driver in a rusted out silver pickup
clips the side of a parked school bus
in front of magic mike's

thankfully nobody is hurt
though a fireman slips in the mud
leftover after a january ice storm

everything is melted
the driver is screaming at the county sheriff
about just wanting to go home

the former mayor looks like he needs a nap
as he tries to put the mailbox back in the ground
while they take her away in cuffs.

Poem for J.P.

i don't know how many pairs of glasses you lost
how many retainers fell off lunch trays
never to be seen again

these are myths we rarely speak of now

like the ketchup packages we used to launch
off cafeteria tables
that would sail through the air
& land in the hoodies
of other unsuspecting kids

the last time i saw you
it should have been snowing
your own son sat beside you in a booth coloring
while struggling to finish his chicken fingers
even with your help

your laugh was sincere
but you looked tired
for the first time
in over 30 years

talking about your own father
& the tent we used to sleep in
in your backyard

& your mother's pinto
with its rusted out passenger side
where you had to hold your feet up
while driving to the grocery store
as if you were in an episode of the flintstones

it all feels a bit like time travel now
it's almost like it happened to someone else
better versions of ourselves
who would always burn longer
than the sun.

Wolfgang

was raised by his grandfather
on a barren patch of dirt
just up the street from my bus stop
in high school he dated a girl
with thick glasses & a mouth like a dying volcano
who worked second shift with my mom
at the local wendy's

they'd scream at each other
& then make up
just as loudly
behind the dumpster
out back

after graduation rehearsal
we went out into the woods
to smoke a joint
when he told me
that last summer she'd been pregnant
until he threw her down the stairs
but that it was really for the best

he had a short temper & a long bloodline

the trees made him feel small
like he was drowning in an inch of bathwater
& that he would've left already
if he could.

Caroline Haiku

your skin is a nervous yellow
like a dying sunflower
in the toledo morning.

Coco Malone is a Bad Bitch
for jen dayton

before jen moved to brooklyn
she had spent the summer on robinwood
drinking red wine & squealing in italian
every time her boyfriend
ran his hands down her back

telling us all about rome
how it made her feel
like a different person

the sun felt different
her heart felt different
her dreams felt unexplainable

fear had become an inextinguishable fight song
she had to commit to canvas

she was more than one thing
more than one place

she was a dark corner
on cherry street
in the bowery

she said coco malone
would only come out at night
she was a bad bitch

she said they would only dance together
for a few heated seconds

that she was both of them
in a screaming match with herself

that you could never be sure
which one would greet you
in the morning.

Toledo Girls

bridget can't walk without shaking
but i still love her
caroline smells like rose petals
& southern comfort
but i still love her
jessica can't have children
but i still love her
tall jen has multiple personalities now
& i love all of them equally
little jenni isn't whole without a bottle of wine
but i still love her
sarah jayne won't stay in one place
long enough to let me love her
but i still love her.

The End of the Line

my dad's uncle dave would sit in his bedroom
rolling cigarettes & talking to truckers
on his hand built crystal radio
he was always that friendly voice
on the other end of the line

his universe was a long haul
on a short wave

when he went out
he'd check payphones for quarters
everywhere he went
& wipe out arcade claw machines
with a surgeon's steady grip
selling stuffed animals & worthless trinkets
at the flea market every sunday

he taught me how to build my own radio
from a $6 kit i bought
at the local electronics store
because i wanted to talk to the dead

cleopatra
napoleon
billy the kid
lee harvey oswald
liberace
lawrence welk

they were all still out there somewhere
listening for signs of life
in western pennsylvania

when my great aunt leona lay dying
in a hospital bed tossing & turning
as it rained outside her window
all she wanted was to see him again
to have him hold her hand
through the fog of silence
to hear his voice
rolling down the highway
toward anyone
who would listen.

Birthday Poems for the Dead
for frank t. rios

it's always your birthday now

this isn't a poem for the dead

they wouldn't get it

refuse anything they offer you

& help me light another candle

love is holding out for more.

Your Daughter's Country

my grandmother's father
once owned hundreds of acres of land
teeming with corn & cattle
tobacco & a dozen children that he left behind
just after the depression hit
he met my great grandmother
working as a ranch hand for her father
somewhere in west virginia or pennsylvania

the family history gets a little fuzzy

it wasn't until i was in my 20's
that i found out that he had also been
an alcoholic
a railroad man
& a rapist

something my own father never even knew

forced by her father to stay put
after she got pregnant
bearing him several more children
who looked like the milkman
the postal carrier
the trash collector
any one of them made for better company
on a cold night
as he was off riding the rails

they never married
but after he died
they gave her a pass
to ride the train
anywhere she wanted

she never used it
it all seemed like dark country
with its abandoned children
left like tumbleweeds
grasping at straws
for their own mongrel bloodline

there was never anywhere for her to go

that was far enough away
from where she'd already been.

My Grandmother's Half Sister

lived less than a mile
from where we'd vacation
when i was a kid

i only ever met her the once
her skin was cracked
from hours spent
in the blazing sun

i liked to pretend she was a lizard
as she sipped a glass
of home brewed sweet tea

her mouth was shaped like china
commemorating the dust bowl

her teeth almost seemed
to blow away in the breeze
every time she laughed.

Aunt Mary

my uncle jerry
lived with the same woman
for over 20 years
without ever giving her a ring

she had a tenth grade education
& a laugh like a hyena

she would eat $20 worth of burger king
as long as it came with a diet coke
& threatened to stab any woman
who looked in his direction

every time i would walk
into my grandparents house
my grandfather would laugh & say
aren't you happy to see your aunt mary?

i would just glance in her direction
& then quickly look away
before her daggers had a chance
to stab me too.

We Were Still Brave Then

when my grandfather was laid off
in the winter of 1986
my cousin amanda & i stayed up
with flashlights under a blanket
counting our money

a whole $8 between us
we stuffed it into an envelope
& put it on the kitchen table downstairs
with a note written with a dull crayola crayon
about how we just wanted to help out

now i get scared
when my bank account
dips below $100

thinking about toledo
when i wouldn't eat
for 3 or 4 days at a time

but we were braver then
when anything over $5
seemed like it could solve
all of the world's problems

in the morning
my grandfather hugged both of us
before giving us our money back

A few days later
the space shuttle challenger exploded
fast & furious & brilliant
& as i went outside
majesty just seemed
to turn into dirty snow

& even the stars
seemed to have
their limits.

Poem for Mary Anthony

mary says that you won't find god
in the stacks of books
we have piled high
in the bookstore in town

she was a trucker
before she moved back
to open up the only motel for miles
all that time on the highway
if she couldn't find him
out under the stars
what chance do we have?

Gasconade Haiku

the sun is a radical lover
a racist moon
turned pale.

First Impressions of Belle, Missouri

as a kid
my cousin & i spent summers in a trailer
in west virginia
with no running water

we would bathe in the sunlight
in a large steel drum
used to feed cattle in the 1930's

there was no valor in poverty

there were no ghost stories
about dead indians buried in the hills

i had to come here
for that.

Tommy

my great uncle tommy
was born with cerebral palsy
just like me

one of the sweetest men
i've ever known
he was a large baby
big enough to swallow
whole japanese tourists
in some infant godzilla scenario

while i was the size of a minnow
so small they almost threw me back

the only boy
he never left his mother's side
until the day
they put her in the ground
& he spelled her name out in rose petals
on a cheap pine box
that held all the family secrets

The War at Home

as my aunt victoria kicked around
in my grandmother's stomach
the war raged in vietnam
& boys like my father
waited by the mailbox
for death sentences.

His Summer Place

my grandfather's side business painting houses
went south just long enough
for him to lose a piece of property
that had been in our family
since the turn of the century

it was supposed to be his summer place
even though he worked
no matter what season it was

he always said
you have to stay busy

you can't paint
the town red
without a little blood.

White Castle on New Year's
for alex nielsen

i gave alex my last $6
when he offered to go
on a food run just after 3 am

an hour later he came back
covered in fresh bruises & soiled snow
telling me he'd been jumped
by a couple of guys
on the way home

he said they took his money
his french fries & his crave case
of pulled pork sliders

but that he'd managed to hide
my bag of chicken rings
deep inside his bookbag

they were soggy
& tasted like heartburn
& the desperation of winter
along collingwood blvd
but we tapped two together anyway
as if they were filet mignon
& cheersed to another new year
in toledo.

Dressing a Deer in Yellow Springs, Ohio
for jeff west

jessica kept complaining
about wanting taco bell
until we got in jeff's car
in the middle of the night
5 or 6 stoned college girls
piled high on top of each other
in the back seat

jeff turned on his headlights
& we heard a sudden thud
noticing a bleeding deer
attempting to run
into the treeline before collapsing

all of the girls started screaming
i covered my ears
& jeff just stopped the car
popped the trunk & got out
coming back with a shotgun
to finish it off

he threw the deer & the gun
back in the trunk

A few miles down the road
we ordered in silence

& headed back to their dorm
where jeff made squeamish vegan girls
help him carry in the lifeless thing
to the nearest sink still dripping blood
he taught them how to dress a fresh kill
later making venison stew
while everyone else
quietly ate their burritos.

Belle the Musical

in the dining room of the dinner belle
everyone gives love a bad name
waitresses & camouflage covered farmers
shout out bon jovi lyrics
like they're reciting hamlet

he never went through anything
like the struggles
they face every day

in the kitchen
the cook flours
a small mountain of chicken
before throwing it into the fryer
& shakes her ass
as prince comes on the radio
stopping every few seconds
to make a kissing sound
with her lips.

Poem for Larry Gawel

it's hard to find a direct positive
for thin skin
in a fair weather town

history is unpredictable

religion is a hitching post
for comfort food

this town has a sign that says
get settled in.

What's Left of Love

for mark shaffer

isn't buried in a flower garden
in your backyard
or on the lips of a minister
who couldn't get your wife's name right
through the entire service.

On Water Street

as we sat in the diner
across from my friend terry's old studio
counting out loose change
to pay for a single plate of toast & eggs
they found a body floating behind the building

ask anyone
it's sink or swim in north toledo
even if all you're trying to do
is cross the river styx
one final lap
at a time.

When Terry was in Rescue Crisis

there was this guy
who claimed to have been
on star search in the winter of 1984
just like in life
nobody ever remembers
the runner up

instead they ask you
for your last cigarette

before you wander off
to a better time.

Me & Bobby Mcgee

for kris kristofferson & caroline gauger

i'm sure that song
was written for a girl in toledo

with fiery red hair
who sang you to sleep
on a warm summer night.

Dean

my dad's cousin dean
could raise his lip
like elvis presley

he was the king
of western pennsylvania
but couldn't sing a lick.

From Memory

after my grandfather went blind
he had my grandmother
take him to get
his driver's license renewed

& snuck out to his truck
as fast as his prosthetic leg
would carry him

somehow he got in
& drove into town from memory

& right off the side of a little bridge
& into the icy cold creek water

the policeman who found him
just had the family come take him home
without reporting anything

on the way there he remembered
how he used to shoot from the foul line
& danced circles around those jokers
at his high school prom

now he had to do everything
from memory.

Poem for Oscar on a Life Well Lived

my great uncle oscar
was named after his father
who dropped dead
of a heart attack at the age of 52
just after the second world war

he drove stock cars at the local track
well into his 80's
& when he laughed
his love for his wife
showed all over his face.

River People

for andrew tucker

our people come from the hills of shenandoah
& the rivers of pittsburgh

if you've ever seen a paper sailboat
burn up from the inside

then you know trash flows evenly
no matter where you throw it

dirty water is dirty water.

Andrew

i wonder if my grandmother looked like you
i wonder if i have your eyes or your nose
i wonder if you ever rode the same rails
where neal cassady watched his final sunset
with a bottle in his hand.

The Ballad of Emilie Rose

your life wasn't exactly a sad song
you got married
raised a family
& talked to the dead
through the mouths of butterflies
who promised to never fly away.

The Afterlife of the Party
(Ragged Lion Press, 2019)

Where the Prom Queen Ends Up or
Poem for Kristen

there is nobody waiting outside
the cowboy cafe & truck stop
to bring you flowers
or even offer you their coat
on a rainy afternoon
in lyman wyoming

most mornings you are
the first thing the sun sees
no matter when you punch in
& time stands still just long enough
for you to remember
how you ended up here

how this was just supposed to be a summer job
how calendars can bend the will of any ambition
how your thighs were once a temple of worship

stray dogs still sniff your ass
for that last scent of beauty
for that last slice of cherry pie
made holy by your touch

at least once a day
you are still
the most beautiful woman in the world
depending on who you ask

& if the wind kicks up just right
in any direction
you are still magic.

Creatures of Our Better Nature

as i stop to watch the gossip of a bluebird
through a dirty glass window
i think it is november
& i'm sipping champagne
on a half built deck
in the woods
that may never get finished

just me & some lonely bluebird
fluttering our wings
like crazed teenagers
mauling each other
in front of some steamy glass sunset
on some makeout mountain
that even time
can't look away from

for a few seconds i am that bird
& that bird is me

& we are both beautiful here

when all at once
the sun wraps its fingers
around our throats
& begins to sing.

The Goats in December

the goats across the way are crying
sunlight is not the same thing as empathy
or brown grass in the middle of winter

the river has a lovely singing voice
when you place your hand
over its mouth.

At Padgett's Place

sitting in the pool hall
in the middle of the afternoon
is as good a use of my time as any

one day they might name a sandwich after me

some people name stars after dead lovers
& go to sleep hungry

you can't swallow a comet

i'm better off here

where there is a sandwich made for hustlers
where paul newman's ghost smiles
at the first pretty girl he sees

time is the true love of all worried men
chalk outlines on their lips

we are all skating on small ponds

the jukebox is the closest thing
to therapy there is
& it always seems
like a better idea
than going home.

Huck in Old Age

as curly sits playing keno
he offers me a shot of hot damn
while telling me how last summer
he took a group of writers out on his boat
& mentions that he doesn't really even like to read

but he has a sense of adventure

he is huck decades later
searching for becky thatcher
from the same barstool almost every night

the fog is thick in his mind
but he is still the closest thing to mark twain
franklin county has on a tuesday afternoon

o sweet becky thatcher
i can feel the heat
coming off of his glass
every time
he mentions your name.

Another Reason Why I Love This Town

on any given day of the week
you might see a woman
in a bathrobe chasing a german shepherd
on the grass outside the post office

you might say that she
was almost beautiful once
& she might have been

it might have been a wednesday
& she might have been
listening to neil young
sing about the moonlight
while getting that tattoo on her ankle
down the street from some campus bar
a lifetime away from where she is right now

her dog pissing out what looks like
a whole pitcher of flat budweiser
its foaming head watering the lawn
marking its territory
on the past.

Gasconade Bloodlines

one farm over they have been
tilling the land for days
if there was a pond
maybe the dead would skim pebbles
across the skin of the soil
but everything here is more blood
than water

thin as tomato soup
& generations old

the moonlight rarely offers any hope
all bones begin their lives
as dirt.

Poem for Donald Lev

you were like something out of the movies
with your working class bare white knuckles
fingers wrapped tight around whiskey bottles
the wife you adored
& all of poems you ever wrote

you were the last honest man
at any party

you always knew
when it was time to go.

Poem for Felino

i wonder who found your body
who tapped the last bit of jazz
out of your ears

trapped in there like a hornet
like a ghost born again

building castles out of bone.

Questions for Marlon Harris

who would play you in a movie
pam grier or mata hari

why were you always coughing

why is death the sun's favorite color

when your heart stopped
where did the love go?

Wendy Has Never Marched on Selma

has never fought for anything
never listened to bloody sunday
& knew what it meant
in her bones

she's never looked past the blood
never prayed for the humanity
of anne frank
& emmett till

in the same breath

she just sits in the kitchen
calling martin luther king jr.
the loudest nigger they could find to shoot
instead of the gentle freedom fighter he was

she has never known
the inside of the heart
never known the equality
that comes with love

the whole time she's been talking
she has never once glanced up
from her phone long enough
to look us in the eye.

Free as a Bird

for eric roetter

the image i have
in my heart
is you flying
through city streets
on your bicycle

before daylight
before heroin

the birdman of broad street

i'll tell ya brother
you were already pure.

Anthony Bourdain Crosses the River of the Dead

& there is nothing to eat
a mouse carrying a ham sandwich died
in the corner of the room

its stomach full with pride

but that seems like centuries ago
when mice did things like that
when the outline of a young mother's thigh
could evoke the holy spirit

when we were all the afterlife of the party

when all of our hungry closets got fed
when love danced around
every corner
of our heart

with no reservations.

The Ballad of Pegleg & Double Stamp

as we drop him off at the greyhound
crazy mark says that the whole country is on fire

just outside the station
a legless vietnam vet asks a young girl
where she got her tattoos done

& i think maybe she's a prostitute
or maybe she just looks like his daughter

or the high school sweetheart
he left on prom night
to wander into a jungle
of regret

that's the thing about flames
you can move in any direction
& still end up
in places you never
intended to go.

On or at the Frontier

we make this wilderness
with our own hands
needles left hidden
behind bathroom mirrors
buffalo turned into hamburger
on store bought grills
as children dance
around an empty swimming pool
that was drained
back when johnny carson was king
of late night memories

the night is full of wild wolves
at 7 am even the prostitute in room 16
will soak her tired back in the bathtub
& try to dream

putting out her cigarette
waiting for the sun
to pour through the window
like honey
like a warm pillow

queens & bees die alone
in this town
where the cold kills everything
it doesn't touch.

Poem for Edward Gehlert

there are birds singing outside my window
they don't know that there were nights
when there were no books in your room

mine either

they don't know that there were nights
when your heart was shaped
like a broken dinner plate

because some traditions
have dark designs

forget their values

nobody ever told us
that there are easier ways
to die inside

nobody ever said
that the dead
came back as birds

that felt lucky
to be able
to sing
at all.

Passing Through Leadwood

for daniel crocker

just off the ferlin husky highway
i think what would richard hugo
say about this town
that you haven't screamed
in your sleep
a thousand times before

fueled by wonder bread & poison
sad songs about tradition & empty storefronts
the ghosts that go away quietly
because they know
that they won't be missed

the buildings that crumble
& just slip away
from their foundations

the houses that look normal
the regret that is bought
& paid for
in generations of blood

where the sky is a rusted satellite dish
a dirty diaper on the sidewalk
next to the high school

you & icarus are famous here
like ferlin husky on the wings of a dove

traveling through the body like cancer

on its way to somewhere else

some far away land

where there is nothing to do
but sing.

The Gasconade River is a Metaphor for Your Life

for greg edmondson

it doesn't even have to be a river

really anything that won't dry up

sweat pressed into a notebook
in the shape of a leaf

a girl you once loved
memories that sink like stones

only dead armadillos
are listening for fireflies & heartache

all family histories feel crooked
after a night of clumsy lovemaking
with an ocean that doesn't want
what you have to give.

A Ghost is an Unforgiving River

at forty-one
i've learned that we're only as fast
as what we can outrun

that my legs were rubber bands
in another life
the product of a war
i'll never win

a foreign body of water
an unforgiving river

memories only immigrate
to other parts of the brain

other borders of the heart
that never close

blood rarely changes course

rarely does the right thing

when you expect it to.

On a Lazy Summer Day

dead skin scatters
like dandelion seeds
across the hilltop
& i think about the year
i turned 12

about the 2 teenage girls
who were abducted
& killed walking home
from the video arcade
near my grandmother's house

it was all over the news

that was the summer
my mother ran out of quarters
because playing pacman felt dangerous

& the other kids who walked by that street
would swear up & down
that there were ghosts
guiding them home to safety

i think about how
i wanted to be out there
walking a thin line
amongst the spirits

about how we do things just because
we want to belong to something

to anything

that makes us believe
in magic.

Rosalea Ain't Dead Yet

for victor clevenger & michael hathaway

in front of the st. john courthouse annex
we notice a bumper sticker
on the back of a minivan

rosalea ain't dead yet

she stands there in tears
punching numbers into the sun
like a holocaust survivor
she once met here as a girl

like a ghost
like a relic
like a tumbleweed
like a bomb
going off
in her heart

like a religion
like a miracle

while in harper kansas
they plaster posters on trees
plant nooses around the necks of sunflowers

red tulips are painted gray

glass blown out of the windows

in front of her hotel
in front the old anchor oyster parlor

black birds & gas station girls
ask if we are famous
& rosalea pulls a blanket over her head
to keep out the moonlight

the prairie connection

nothing is sacred here
but time

& rosalea ain't dead yet

and the red sea
was once a wheat field
a burning building
meant to raise the dead

& rosalea ain't dead yet

she ain't dead yet

until the prairie
comes & takes
her very last breath

takes her tongue
takes everything

that hasn't somehow
already blown away.

Couch Poem

this couch smells watergate
like linda lovelace's worst fears
like billie jean king in her prime
after a whole afternoon spent broiling in the sun
on a warm spring day

this couch smells like the gas shortage
like an unpaid mortgage
like a failed marriage
like a key party
where everyone came on foot
like the iran hostage crisis
like high school sweethearts
who will never find true love again

this couch had lunch with jimmy hoffa
this couch knows
where all of the bodies
are buried
& it isn't
telling anyone.

Getting Lucky

for jason ryberg & matthew haines

on a cold missouri morning
my pockets smell of spring air
& day old marijuana
the sunflower of the south

pulled over & frisked by the county sheriff
before i've even had a chance
to brush my teeth

i think about the first girl i ever loved
running her fingers along the seams
of my $13 walmart trousers

for a few moments i forget where i am
forget the order of the things
& let the universe
run its fingers along my asshole
just long enough to let the sun in.

Prostate of the Union

for daniel crocker

it isn't about what's shutdown
it's about opening your heart
it's about carol channing
in a warm bathrobe
childhood crushes
& conducting musicals
in the missouri moonlight

every journey is a close shave
it's about just finding your footing
no matter where
you call home.

Lean

erica says
those must have been lean years
as she hands me $40 in a bar parking lot
for some books
in the middle of winter

like a drug deal
where nobody gets high

years spent reading in smoke filled bars
until time stopped

years when i stopped
to check my empty pockets
for music almost every night
walking home downtown
or along the greenbelt

years of not eating all day
& going home alone

yeah it was a party

not much has changed.

Bridget

our timing was all wrong
like a busted cuckoo clock

you tell me that the yoga is working
that you haven't had a drink in years

but you shake like a willow tree
that i want to wrap my arms around.

Dying Like Dogs
(Tangerine Press, 2018)

Dying like Dogs

even as a kid
i can remember
that my mother's sister
could never let go of anything
spending thousands to
to keep a dying german shepherd alive
for a few more months

a beagle for a few more fleeting weeks

& now sitting outside
drinking iced tea
on a warm spring day
my mother says that she
is thinking about making me
the family executor

it's not because of the cold killer instinct
that i jokingly claim to have
that thing that pennsylvania winters
just seem to instill in you at birth
like having to let your favorite sports teams hopes
go out with the frost

it's only that my father
is not a labrador

& she is not a teacup poodle
no matter what her latest haircut
might lead you to believe

it's just that they
don't want to die
like dogs.

The Postman Never Screams Twice

for Annie Menebroker

it lasted all of a weekend
heartbeats turned to flesh
tapped out on skeleton keys
& the bones of underwood typewriters
there was some silly argument
that sent you running into the eye of the storm
sitting there in tears
on wine soaked sidewalks
all suitcases & no destination
waiting on a bus
with youthful fire
him, not yet a lion
& you, hardly a timid creature
he walked outside
& pleaded with you
to come out of the rain
nuzzling your face
looking into your eyes
like they were empty six packs
full of nothing but moonlight

like a love letter never sent
you were too real
for anything
this close to sunset blvd

years later your spirit is still running
in every direction
saying, hey, baby
a little rain never hurt anyone.

In Kansas Thinking of You

for cherie

ted berrigan would never text
with his fingers
along your skin
he would call you
to borrow some money or pills
he would give you some story
about how the moon looks beautiful
while sipping a pepsi
he would use strong words
& dance nude with donna dennis
on your parents front lawn
they, your parents, would offer him
iced tea & cucumber sandwiches
while talking about the moon landing
about how it seemed like a lot of work

you would sit there in flower patterned pajamas
while he told you that you deserve to have words
wrapped around you like oak trees

& all i have to offer you is the kansas wind
something of the earth
my own thoughts on love
which i know isn't much.

The Patriotic Gutters of Purcell, Oklahoma

the museums of the dead
were built for small corners like this
dust covering the highways
once kicked up by horses
made of bronze and flesh
where they remember the wars
but forget the bones

forget the ghost dancers
who once thumbed a ride
to wounded knee

forget the half built railroads
that cluttered the hearts of men

forget the blood
on the hands of young lovers
who died so we could hold hands
in the moonlight

because romeo & juliet
refused to throw rocks at the sun

running into half empty gas stations
in search of day old barbecue

while the dead swing chicken bones

in the rain like the warriors
they once were

while the half starved dogs
we imagine ourselves to be
become skeletons in the night air

saying

save yourselves

there are saints
buried under your feet.

Tammy Talks Tough

tammy storms into the pool hall
screaming about how
she's been driving around
on one lug nut

saying that she knows
that her ex-boyfriend
is trying to kill her

she squeezes her fists
wrapping her dreams
around a warm bottle of stag
& the cool silence of nights like these

saying that he used to make her feel tender
every time they slow danced
to johnny ace on the jukebox
she pledged her love

but now the only song
that touched her lips
was dead man's curve

but that that was alright
he would get his

she said that her current boyfriend pickle
had fixed her car himself
& that he knew his way around a lug nut
and all of the tattered edges
of her heart.

Tammy Practices the Art of Negotiation
in Rolla, Missouri

a weary mechanic walks
into the waiting area
of the walmart automotive center
he shakes his head at tammy
as he tells her that he can't
patch her tire again
that it's more patch than rubber
at this point

wiping sweat from his forehead
he says that it's a lot like a broken heart
some things just can't be fixed
until you let them die
on their own

when he tells her
they can get her
a used tire for $58

all of the air seems
to go out of her face
& there is no patch for that either

she gets on her cell phone
small child by her feet
playing with a plastic dump truck

as if predicting his working class future
she negotiates a blowjob with an ex-boyfriend
playing with her dirty blonde hair
pretending to giggle as she fights back tears
pretending that tires
always get you
where you want to go.

Damsels in Detroit
(Indigent Press, 2018)

More Tattoos than Teeth

the only general store in town
is enough to prove
that darwin
was a charlatan

that there are places
where time stands still

where nothing evolves
into a flower

where the gas pump
is always busted

where even a monkey
could make correct change.

Sunrise is a Fragile Lover

the sky lit up
with heaven's misguided bloodlines.

No Phone Booths

there are no more phone booths
no super heroes changing
into better versions of ourselves
no bones held together
by the whims of stable genius
no religious wars
built on faith
in long goodbyes

the wind blows hard
when there are no stars.

Puberty Was a Fever Dream

in pittsburgh we had our idols
donnie iris
chipped ham sandwiches
joe denardo predicting
one hundred years of solitude
and settling out of court
for six more weeks of winter

while i scribbled in a sweaty notebook
bring me the head of larry levis
i want to dream his dreams

somewhere a young girl still dances
at her prom with myron cope
it's a slow song
about the value of hard work.

Old Greg is a Rooster

half a bottle of lunazul tequila
& the cool night air
brushing against your past
feels like a handjob
from the ghost of evan williams.

Scott Wannberg Nearly Broke My Hand
in a Stockon Denny's

somewhere between stockton
& the ends of the earth
we huddled to piss
in an empty orange grove
spring air wafting up

just standing there
no snow under our feet

just after 3 am
miles stacked up
like bones.

John Berryman Diving School

my sonnets about rivers
could never match
the babble of your dreams

your form was perfect
all the way down
to the rocks.

It's a Wonderful Life, Somewhere

the postman is rosy cheeked
from bourbon or the winter chill

the air tastes like gingerbread & meth.

George Bailey Doesn't Live Here

all day i listen to the sound of sirens
& think about love like a controlled burn
the youth we abandon in rusty train cars
our angels buried
in unmarked graves.

Outlaws & Burned Out Bookstores:
A Detroit Poem

in the middle of the afternoon
there is nothing left to steal but words
hymns for an invisible god

jesse james would've just shot his horse
& ran away on foot.

Fake News, Real Blues

we skim facts like pebbles
across the osage river
the maumee the cuyahoga
still burning for truth
the forgotten tributaries of sacred dreams
of all the shithole countries
growing in our hearts
that we would kill to defend.

The Ugly Side of the Lake
(NightBallet Press, 2018)

At Popeyez Bar & Restaurant

the only server goes to topeka
every other week
telling her son
that they live
on the ugly side of the lake

she looks like a chloe or a tammy
not wynette or anything resembling debbie reynolds
with her 1950s farm fresh charms
but a prom queen who never stopped dancing
to 80s hair metal

as you look out the window
mist comes off the water
& the beer tastes as warm
as her lips.

At Oscar's Classic Diner

our waitress is a hummingbird
though she claims to be an idiot
her self esteem
worth less than a check
for day old cherry pie

even after we assure her
that there's no such thing
as the wrong gravy.

At the Glory Hole

they burn prospects for warmth
the only woman here
could be your grandmother
if she sold her teeth to pay the rent

the beer tastes like a watery grave

the only sexual position
is room temperature or none at all

the fist pumps always come shit faced

the bathroom is strangely clean
no holes to speak of
& all of the glory
washed away
years ago.

J & J's Café on a Sunday Afternoon

in town for less than 2 weeks
jeff mentions for the fifth time
that he was at stevie ray vaughan's funeral
as if touching death will make him famous

he says it was a warm day
he says that stevie wonder cried

he complains that we have no dinner rolls
that they're treating us like tourists
that nobody here has any respect
for the dead.

Linzi

points to a road sign off the highway
saying don't you wish
you knew who wilbur wright was

it's late

you think to yourself
maybe she never learned to fly

maybe she traded her history books
for a smartphone

but it's too dark out now
to answer existential questions of the soul
while pissing behind
an empty gas station.

In This Heat
(CWP Collective Press, 2018)

Moon Over Eufaula, Oklahoma
for victor clevenger

just south of muskogee
dumpster cats guard crumbling pyramids
& discarded bbq grills
in the moonlight

the creek nation girls still dance
in honor of their own virginity
covered in dust
& humble bones
yelling free bird lives

free bird lives

here everyone is loyal
& your breath just hangs there
as heavy as a cloud

& apartments are shaped
like tombstones

& the outline of a girl's hips
in the shadow of a lonely gas station
can still transport you back
to a better time.

Poem For Denis Johnson

every morning
i'd sit on the steps
of the university
while jesus' son filmed
across the street

billy would stop by
and tell me
about fetching breakfast burritos
for angry movie stars

there was no lens there
to capture his pain
as he talked about
getting the orders wrong
for the 12th time in 2 weeks
before getting up to start the day
all over again

redemption stories
weren't meant to start at 6 am
on a tuesday.

Diabetes Poem

it makes me think about jaws
how i wish fate
would just swallow me whole

before circling
for blood.

Poem for Denis Johnson #2

sometimes we're all a little lost
but the sunrise
isn't just about overcoming
an addiction to darkness.

A Tow Truck Named Desire

stars scream out into the night
somewhere on the muddy side streets of our hearts
where the universe has always depended
on the kindness of strangers

crying out-

is it okay now
to die inside?

Mythology Begins With Fire

van gogh, slice a tip off the moon
call it your ear
your mountains will never turn to blood

bravado is inarticulate
a generation of crows
will never dream about sunflowers

while the night
you've dreamt of
refuses to burn.

On Eva's Birthday
for annie menebroker

we drank red wine

ate flourless chocolate cake
for cardio

sunlight beamed
like a commodity

our hearts grew strong
with love.

Goat Song

most mornings
it isn't about
being able to carry a tune

death sounds the same regardless.

Rocky Mountain Poem

the car nearly didn't make it
traffic stalled out

i'm not some silly sentimental asshole
but at a certain altitude
i miss you more than air.

Peter Pan in Carhartts

they have lost boys everywhere
the trees are full of them.

Spiders the Size of Dogs

a dead hawk lying in the sun

in this heat
it's hard to remember
where you left your heart

& nobody is going
to draw you
a map.

Lew Welch Returns From the Woods

lew of the chicago morning
fireball of youth

ferlinghetti's tired shotgun
brushing away the sun
from your eyes
to face

the morning rush.

Lew Welch Returns From the Woods #2

lew maybe you were just sleeping
for more than 40 years
the sound of crashing waves
muffling history's alarm clock
baby huey spreading the news
on a dime store radio

packing several lifetimes
into one dusty sack.

Lew Welch Returns From the Woods #3

lew you hiked the entire expanse of the human heart
expecting your friends would be waiting on the other side
the meaning of life was a river you could never cross alone

if only someone had told you
that love was rugged terrain.

Heart

my grandmother used to walk
five miles every day
in cheap canvas shoes
she'd buy from the five & dime
by the gross

they don't make things
like they used to

even our bones are outsourced
snapping under their own weight
in $100 loafers.

Poem for Todd

i can still hear dillinger
calling you in from the tall grass

& billie spraying you
right in the kisser
with dandelions

& you thinking
is this what bullets feel like?

Glass City Lolita

at 26 i was in love with a 17 year old girl
who brought me oranges & chocolate cake

& sleepless nights

humbert humbert
with much less success.

At New Derry Theater

someone had spray painted
mr. rogers was a straight edge
along the side entrance

frankie & doug talked about shakespeare
as couples made out
with hardcore bands
rumbling in the background

i came up with and then forgot
the greatest poem ever written
at least fifteen times that night
the way you do at seventeen

all i could remember
is that i was in love.

The Midwestern Guide to Time Travel

for mark shaffer

remember to dance in a 10 ft. steel cage
one for every year of your life

to dream of a future
filled with flying cars
and international date lines
that seem as limitless
as homespun wisdom

somewhere a little voice
tells you to drown a mermaid
in 39 ft of water or a hill of dirt

it sings for blood
as the sun
touches your skin.

Hey Joe

auden never sang a funeral dirge
for a dog buried in the woods
his heart resting
under the weight of joy
13,000 bricks

a child's shoebox
can become a time machine
or a proper tombstone
if you let it

like the song says
where you gonna run now, where you gonna go?

it's pretty cool

thinking about your tail
wagging at every stranger
you'll never meet
in harmony

before your ashes turn to stardust
guarding ronnie's feet
and mix with the earth.

Godless Animals
(Analog Submission Press, 2018)

Godless Animals

for richard hugo

you gave humanity
to nameless streets
savage winters
landscapes built on regret
as real as the face
of a beautiful girl
who once loved this town
with all her heart.

In 1954

my grandmother was beautiful
this country had white teeth
& a red scare

we elected bravado
& admitted nothing

we painted houses
with the blood
of immigrants
& called it pride

our dreams were real
& our scars
were still fresh.

Braddock Serenade

my father says
that he thinks my grandfather
had bunch of mini heart attacks
years before we knew
his health went south
but just kept going
like the energizer bunny
covered in factory dust
& pittsburgh moonlight

i just remember his smile
how it glowed
playing through the pain
feeding sadness into the mouth
of bellowing smokestacks
boilers of generational poverty

the blood of the roman dead
covering his work boots
staining his dentures
taking away everything
it could.

What Independence Meant in Irwin, Pennsylvania

at a certain point
you start thinking
about everything
in terms of the past

you view winter with nostalgia
until snow nearly melts in your hands
you say it wasn't there
never happened
until summer was only your grandparents
filling the car with illegal fireworks
from winchester virginia
to shoot off on the lawn
& over the roof of the house
in a cloud of smoke
with hotdogs and potato salad
your can of pepsi was never empty then

even as a child
you were told
that someday
all of this
would seem
like magic.

The Mark Twain Speech
for mark mcclane

you talk about frontiers
that only dead men
& drunks can see

not about the blood
& sweat that goes
into words that won't sell
the stories of heartbreak
& what time can do
to beautiful things
everything turned to bone

words careening off your tongue
& down a river
slow to offer amnesty
to those in a sinking ship.

The Boy from Bartlesville

prophets were born and raised here
their bones in the pipeline of the past
when each man was his own tribe

when the lenape cried out
in the sunlight
for mother's milk

after the jug of the spirit
had gone empty

when the boy from bartlesville
watched young girls dance
just outside his window
pacing the ward floor
waiting for muhammad
to seek his advice

when invisible prairies still offered
the possibility of young love

when the cosmos was powered
by white bread & gasoline

when wind ripped through these fields
like the last gust of breath from the dead

when nothing sacred
could be held down
by a stone.

Pigpen

rolled tamales
on south street
for $4 an hour
under the table
cash money

it was a slow fix

his next bag of dope
waiting in some west philly squat
it all came from mexico
the tortillas & the black tar salvation

he'd drop by the house on naudain
his hands stiff by end of the day
talking about music and painting
before wandering out under the sky
where nothing was free
but the moonlight
at least came cheap.

Tough Love

a week after his wife's death
crazy mark & i sit on his porch
smoking a joint
in the middle of the afternoon
when he tells me that his niece
mailed him a pocket pussy
from an adult bookstore in arkansas

he tells me at first
that he couldn't figure out
how the damn thing even worked
& that it was barely big enough
to fit a pencil down there.

Ray Gene

the selfish part of me thinks
there's one less friend to call
in the middle of the night now

one more joint that will go unsmoked

one less pussy poem
written in the stars
along cherry street.

Ray Gene #2

who will i talk to about girls?

about sunsets the color of panties

the pearly gates don't deserve you
or your never ending supply of vicodin.

Punk Rock at 45

when i look at your life now
i think nancy spungen got off easy
breast cancer at 45
you have be a fighter
to sleep in the streets
with your broken heart
just dangling there
like a locket made of bones

i remember you at 30
beautiful
tough
& sad

talking about your family
as we drove to 7-eleven
to get hotdogs on christmas eve

how it all came flooding back
your father threatening to drive
the whole family off a bridge
into icy cold arkansas river water
on christmas morning

or the near rape
by a family friend
at fourteen

or the countless bad relationships
that became your anthem
as much as nick cave
or the murder city devils
ever were

your lungs filled up with silence

as the night sky balled up
into a fist
& hurled your childhood
into the past.

Cool like Whip

the first time i ever saw a retarded person
was at the old greengate mall
where years later my brother and i
would drink cheap red wine
on the hill as we watched the cars go by
to busier destinations

terry was in his mid 40's then
his mother would drop him off every morning
placing a crisp $20 bill in his hand
telling him not to lose it every time
reminding him to she'd be there to pick him up
right before they were about to close

he would offer everyone a hug
& a high five
with a smile on his face

there wasn't a security guard or
a food court worker
who he wasn't on a first name basis with

his money spent on glitter covered sunglasses
& backwards baseball caps
bermuda shorts
& giant foam fingers
for local sports teams

if you asked how he was
he'd say cool like whip
& laugh until he was blue in the face
just in case you didn't get the joke

when i heard that his mother died
i wondered who would be there
to pick him up that night
i wondered if there were tears
behind his sunglasses after that
& when someone asked him how he was
i wondered if he said anything at all.

Letting the Meat Rest
(Spartan Press, 2017)

Bugsy Siegel's Desert Rose

lit up in blood
the neon bones of midwestern tourists
streaming in the moonlight

the greeks never knew tragedy like this
shakespeare's quill was filled
with weak ink
& savage glory

sad country songs kneel in protest
woody guthrie's ghost is dreaming
of north korea on a full stomach

the slot machines of change
have gone silent
in their regret

empty parking lots
have run out of luck

this is tom petty's final moment of heartbreak
are you listening?

there is no chorus worth repeating
that isn't about love

so don't even waste your breath.

The Only Thing

for victor clevenger and everette maddox

written down
on the bathroom wall
of the maple leaf bar
is
tell my mother i love her
somewhere the marrow
of our speech
is always
faint praise
& we are all veterans
of some invisible war
but we still need these memories
& plenty of paper towels
to wash our hands.

Nikki, in the Summer Heat

steve & i were looking up at the ceiling
in my studio
like two kids
away at summer camp
when he told me
that you were hiv positive

there were no fireflies
or melting marshmallows
to drown out the silence

no sirens
or broken beer bottles
clamoring like urban wind chimes
in the alley
below my window
just his half deflated 70s air mattress
complete with leopard print
and my broken down office couch
wincing at the thought
that there was nothing
that could repair
the damage.

Nikki, Full of Grace

for steve goldberg and bob phillips

the first time we ever met
you wore sunglasses
in the basement
of an east toledo punk club
where i was reading poetry
in the dark

backed up by a strung out piano player
under a photo of g.g. allin

bob went out to his car
& came back
with a half used jesus candle
from the dollar store

that lit up the room

with outline of your face
thin like a wafer

like the bones
of a half written patti smith song
about the madonna's last days
spent counting the stars
over detroit

the fire in your eyes
burning the fingers of anyone
who dared to touch you.

Degrees of Gray on Ashland Ave

for richard hugo and robert brundage

you might come here
looking for bones
bob brundage's smile winking
a gift from the moonlight
passing through the trees
beneath the roots
he fought so hard for

scott high school on the radio
& chester's fried chicken
sold on the same corner
where i once saw nick muska
search empty bus stops
for a $5 blowjob on his 64th birthday

he had to make it quick
before the candles blew out

on ashland ave
where i once
felt true joy
walking home
from manhattan's
to a room
the size of a prison cell
that cost me 75 bucks a month
& all the sanity i could spare

where upward mobility
meant spaghetti instead of ramen
shared with a punk rock girl
on at least half a dozen
off brand antipsychotics

where nobody has ever loved anyone
as much as they thought was possible
at sixteen

where the heart still aches

while we wait to ask the dead
for their forgiveness

before turning out the lights.

This Street Feels Like Redemption
for ray swaney

the morning comes to you
like a lover
offering no apologies
for its scars

the wind is strange fruit here

the sun beating down
is a crucifixion
not unlike the end
of the world

just a few blocks away
huddled in the rain.

Poem for Ray Patrick

as a kid
you ran girls
white lightning
& stolen boats
up & down the river
of the dead

all along the coast of florida
& the mouth of the maumee

imagining you were huck finn
on acid in the mustard house

drowning in wild irish rose
with etheridge k. & cowboy bob
toasting the sunrise
on the corner of delaware

thirsty for more hell.

Terry at 5150

you swore up and down
that you had seen never never land
from the top of the high level bridge
as i pulled you away from the window
in your studio

going straight to rescue crisis
on a 5150 on the same floor
where debbie had gotten into a fist fight
with another girl
over half a bottle of mountain dew
losing her hallway privileges for good

you swore you'd never get old here
all skin and bones and ramen
you'd rather live on peanut butter
& die on rock n' roll

dancing to buddy holly & bad brains

shaking as i handed you
another lit cigarette.

Gay Marriage in Second Floor Hallway

terry & jeff slept on the floor of a cell room
no bed just a few couch cushions
split between them

no couch

no leftover divinity

no sisters
of mercy
hard at work

terry had just told tom they were a couple
to keep a friend out of cold
on a february night

but that he could prove it
if he had to.

The Real World on Collingwood Blvd.

corey skated through the hallway
in a cotton sundress
on roller skates
covered in glitter

clutching a bottle of cheap red wine
as he yelled
that this was his first time
in the real world.

Jeff Walked In
for nikki

on you fingering your vagina

while injecting heroin

in his bathroom

in a basement apartment

across the street

from scott high school

you said it was the only way

you could get off

it was your cello

your violin

drowning out the sad song

of class bells

like sweet music

to your ears.

Richard's Heart

was as noble as anyone
who was forced to clean out
shower stalls & mop up
the crusty floors
of an ancient porno theater
while living hand to mouth
on music & brown rice.

The Last Voyage of Captain Black

for yusef lateef

joe felt the beat

while you painted tiny hearts
& images of rosa parks
on warped pieces of plywood
in a stolen studio
before marrying the gatekeeper.

Heart like a Loaded Gun

once i was fearless
walking down ashland ave
at all hours

decoding poems in the moonlight
church's chicken in afternoon

two guns pressed against my temples
in broad daylight

they took my rent money
my orange juice
& my dignity

like love everything laid bare
when you least expect it.

High Level Cafe Poem

toast
fried eggs
& overcooked potatoes

can save your life.

Nikki, Last Stand at Murphy's

fired after a single weekend
working as a cocktail waitress
at a legendary jazz club

just hours before
you had begged me
to find you a ride

while fumbling around in your pockets
for a needle

while trying to look elegant
on your hands and knees

after a whole sheet of pills
fell all over the floor of my studio
like a string of pearls.

Marlon

could've been an international spy
for all we knew

she laughed when i called her an enigma
on the corner of baldwin

coughing all over the old west end
a pack of misty's riding on her hip

but if she loved you
she let the world know it.

The Last Days of the Revolution

nick & joel packed into a tiny volkswagen
looking for half a joint
in the cool cleveland evening
zach & i sharing cold cans
of split pea soup
waiting in the bus station

this is what it has come to.

Rodney was Afraid

to have a kid
that's why i waited so long he says
now in his 40s
he points to a framed picture
of his daughter dangling on a loose nail
in the hallway

she could've ended up just like me
he says talking about our days
in a classroom for kids with learning disabilities

he tells me she has a real head for numbers

& here he is with a 9th grade education

afraid now that soon
they'll be coming for our guns

i tell him that the world ended years ago
that they just forgot to tell us

he just laughs

saying that if custer's last stand taught us anything
nobody is getting out of here alive

the numbers just don't add up

& here he is making 80 grand a year

driving a fuel truck in the dead of winter

the bones of sunlight
crushed out under his boot soles

just waiting

for someone

to light a match.

Scott Wannberg as an Old Man

what about those years
you'll never get to see
your poems carved into rocks
or useless cute emojis
or into the hearts of the young lovers
you never were

we don't need love poems anymore, scott
in this last political ice age
we don't need good conversation
warmed over the fire
of silly dreams

what would you say now anyway?
what would they make of your heart?
would they teach it to dance
or stomp it out?

even heartbreak is sold separately
its batteries went out years ago

at least we no longer need to walk
toward the light
to find anything
that makes sense.

Poem for My Aunt on Her Birthday

at 63
you look 80
sound like darth vader
if they had sold menthol cigarettes
on the death star

swollen veins
a cough as big
as a mushroom cloud

you were young once

before diabetes & mental illness
before time became just another broken heart
in a shabby apartment
next to a rundown bowling alley
in a yearbook
full of ghosts

you were young once

put up for adoption
mother hit by a car
like a speeding bullet
father drunk & soon long gone

you were young once

engaged
& cutting hair
in neighborhood salons
around pittsburgh

your sunset was an italian song

about love

given up
&
taken away

one sister married
the other off to college

you stayed home
into middle age

clock ticking in the hallway
watching your hair turn gray
& become a spider web

but you were young once

goddamit you were so young once.

Letting the Meat Rest

a pork chop sizzles in a pan
for six minutes tops
any longer & you'll let the imagination
bleed out all over your plate
& escape into the woods
like magic.

Shoot the Messenger
(Red Flag Poetry, 2017)

The Alligator Man

a bernese mountain dog collects dust
in the living room
as fox news hammers home
the integrity of relics

the sun is just one of a thousand knick knacks
that gets drowned out by the pulse of your love
frozen hamburgers and a bunn coffee maker
hum moonlight melodies
in the middle of the afternoon

a marriage that can no longer walk
on water
gets frozen in time

feeding miracles the size of minnows
to the alligators you once wrestled
but now call lovers

there are no small ponds
just forgotten rivers of intention

just stolen kisses
captured in the night

great love stories
are the things we don't notice
hidden in a cluttered barn

the little things
we keep
to ourselves.

The Prettiest Girl in Moscow, Kansas

pumps gas with a farmer's bicep
and sells off brand energy drinks 2 for $4
tallying the state tax
to determine her own worth
thinking about the prom

when she was queen
of the cattle fields
from here to oklahoma

when the bones of the prairie
sang just for her.

Bone Silo

for annie menebroker

the toughest birds
never even see
the window sill

they dive heart first
into the sun.

Sunny Side Uprising

we peel grease from the sun
wipe our scars from dirty tables
heartbreak is a lit cigarette
dangling

it is just after 7 am
& everything
is on the menu.

Don't Flip the Boat

a drunken hells angel
yells into the mouth
of the river

later claiming his boat
was stolen
in the middle of the night

the insurance company
will buy any yarn
you can spin
he says laughing
guarding its remains
with a shovel
his tongue tastes like
honeysuckle & smoke

the fire of youth
an old tire
left hanging from a tree
that has been burning
since he was a boy

he says there's wisdom
in these hills

he just can't remember
where he buried it.

The Years We Remained Anonymous

waiting for history to moan our names
to carve our initials into a tree
that we can no longer find

the moonlight is no longer happy
just touching the skin of generations
& the road back home
is muddy with blood

there is very little peace

in any of it.

The Loons of Walker Lake

off in the distance
abandoned army barracks
give way to wonder
to what this town once was
bloodlines run deeper than the water now
loons rarely stop to greet the paiute
hovering briefly around the basin
like 1950s ferris wheels with wings
their memories permanently woven
into the sky.

A Town With No Roosters

even the pears are covered with blood
& it makes you wonder
where the chickens came from.

Parker Barrows

out in front of parker barrows deli
i sit smoking a joint
with a self proclaimed outlaw
and a sweet lost kid from indiana

one chasing imaginary bullets
and the other
just trying to find himself

the sun sagging disinterested overhead

both of them dreaming

wounded hawks
in the skyline

ready to fly away
at the first sign
of trouble.

For 35 Years

for justin booth

shooting poison for 35 years
doesn't make you an outlaw

didn't anyone ever tell you
that it takes more courage to dodge a bullet
than it does to curl up
and die with it?

Ladies Night at the Belle Fair

here beauty queens age
in dog years

the hayride lasts
about as long
as their innocence.

Flight Patterns

greg says starlings
are the white trash of birds

it was the woodpecker
that developed morse code.

County Route 705

is full of ghost stories
faded yearbook photos
of dreams that died
on loose gravel

the sun shining
on our failures

just hanging there
like a rusty hubcap
nailed to the cross.

The Colorado Cafe at High Noon

here they tell time by memory
the church down the street is boarded up

an old man wrestles with his youth
and the last piece of day old cherry pie
that seemed destined
for the dumpster out back

fiddle music floats out from the kitchen
the waitress moans about her boyfriend
drunk again
and the death of the silver mines
that once brought money in

the last person here
who spoke her language
is either dead
or long gone.

The Dogs

thrash a kitten
hiding in the shrubs
as the rain comes down
snapping its neck
like a tiny twig
with bones as fragile
as the wind.

Sadie

does yoga under the harvest moon
but has never cried over a lost love
while neil young howls on the turntable

she has never danced backward
into the mouth of oceans
while piecing together the remains
of her tattered heart

her stars still shine through cheap beer
and well whiskey

the highway feels limitless

and the music in her heart seems free.

Home Cooking

my father refused to eat chicken
for more than 40 years
after my grandmother sent him to the hospital
with a stomach full of shake and bake
and a bad case of food poisoning

pizza was always chef boyardee
that tasted just like the box
it came out of

sunday was pepsi and potato chips
deviled salad and chipped ham from isaly's deli
and wondering which one of my uncles
might show up drunk out of his mind

while my grandfather went on
about how my grandmother
had slaved over this meal
as if christ had died
for day old deli meat

hedging our bets
and valuing our stomach lining
we would stop at burger king on the way there

and my grandfather would ask without fail
What's the matter, don't you like your grandmother's
cooking?

i guess it was a fair question
after all, she left a lot of sweat
on that counter.

Killing Two Stones with One Heart

my grandfather taught me how to shoot
by placing my uncles empty beer cans on a tree stump
next to the outhouse in west virginia

with a homemade musket
clay pigeons made from the shrapnel
of genesee cream ale
became the bones of icarus
flying toward the summer sun
before falling
from grace

where we all become myth

killing two stones with one heart

after he died
i wanted three things

a clock with a cheap ruby
in the center
its hands covered
in the blood of hours

that would never turn back time

a photo of him wearing an indian headdress
at the kitchen table
where happiness had turned
to dust

& that musket
pointed at the nostalgia
of paper hearts
under a child's moon
once so full of wonder.

The Rabid Dogs of Winter

In the winter of 1984
mikey stape bit my baby brother
in the side of the face

you might call it frostbite

i bit him back

my mother didn't say a word

because wild packs
look after their own

today we barely speak
we don't have to
in our house
gratitude is a silent season.

The Beautiful People

bob went to my mother's church
he'd worked at the local theater
since the days
of bye bye birdie
& a hard day's night

things never seemed
to get any easier
they rarely do

in his mid forties
he lived with his aging mother
who never had a kind word
for anyone

especially him

on saturday mornings
he taught me
how to thread
the projector
with true human kindness

laughing while talking
about femme fatales
& western tough guys
he could never be

on his nights off
he tooks classes
at the community college

failing a single algebra section repeatedly
for the better part of thirty years

what they never had to teach him
was heart

you are what you project to the world
his mother said looking at his reflection
sideways
through a cracked mirror

beauty leapt out at him
every night
eluding capture
fluttering across the screen
in his heart

he knew things
weren't that black & white
they could always get better
in the next reel

they had to

his dreams
were technicolor.

Rodney Says

the one thing he can't stand are niggers
that the only colors we should be concerned about
are-

RED

WHITE

&

BLUE

we grew up a mile apart
with the same dirt
under our fingernails

he tells me about his heart attack

we have known each other
since we were ten years old
& looking at him now
there is a civil war raging
inside my chest.

Poem for My Parents

for rebecca schumejda

talking about a friend's daughter
my mother reminds me
that i used to bite
people too
whenever i got tired

& that i would pick used chewing gum
off of the floor in shopping malls
screaming at the top of my lungs
whenever she tried to take it from me

& i remind her that she used to do
charcoal drawings of our spirit animals
talking about maybe taking a class
at the community college at some point

that my father got certified in everything
working 60 hours a week
so that i could believe in wonder
as more than just good metaphor
to use in poems
that he'll never read

i remind her
that we are running out of time
that every moment of silence
is another wrinkle on our face
another memory
to hang our bones on.

Cherry Bomb & Boxcar Bertha

for the swogger sisters

cherry & bertha's younger brother chris
accidently shot himself in the head
with their father's favorite hunting rifle
while searching for his christmas gifts
he was never the same after that

all smiles
mixed with fits of rage

nobody died
only his spirit did.

The Rainbow Family Would Never Have You

for david smith

just before sundown
we wandered through the side streets
of your heart
in search of adam's rib
our lips smacking
as we wiped our sticky fingers
on the marrow of dusk

when we were approached by this hippie kid
who asked if you could throw him some gas money
to get to a rainbow gathering in salinas

you frowned when he asked
if i wanted to come along
before handing him a few wrinkled bills
covered in bbq sauce

that's the blood of christ
you said awkwardly laughing
before offering him our leftovers
which he waved away
in a vegan heartbeat
heading toward his bus
while you muttered something
about how it would never
pass inspection anyway

after he had gone
you asked me
why he hadn't invited you
to join in his orgy of drugged-out girls
in tie-dyed t-shirts
with their jam bands & lovely organic hula hoops
three sheets to the wind
running your fingers
through your graying hair
knowing the answer

looking down at your half eaten bbq
you'd be saving the bones for reggie chang
canine king of the jews

reminding me to stay away
from your daughter

nobody was getting lucky tonight, nobody.

.

Poem On My 40th Birthday

poems hide behind mosquitoes
like faded lovers

when there isn't any blood
the river gets fed sweat

wind rips through my ankles
like a bone saw in autumn

my heart has become a heavy ghost

a hawk
crushed
under the weight
of its perch.

Dear Phil

when i was a kid
my mother's best friend
got arrested
for stalking phil collins

she would follow him
around the country
like the grateful dead

she talked about how they exchanged
mad passionate love letters
& how they were going to run away
to their own private island in florida

phil was a great lover
of sunshine and wrestling lyrics
like the alligators of summer

he just couldn't let his female fans know
that his songs were all about her
they'd stop buying his records

we just nodded
when she told us
that we didn't know
how the business worked

the last time she called
was right after hurricane andrew

by then she had left her husband
& was living in florida

phil would be joining her soon
she had written him just last week
he was a great lover, a real giver

& his fingers ran through her hair

like sunshine
beaming
through the clouds.

Harvey Korman, Harvey Korman,
Harvey Korman (Spartan Press, 2017)

The Stigmata of Crazy Mark

your sleeves rolled up
cigarette dangling from
your lower lip

as blood flows
down your arms
with pride

after a morning spent
banging a chainsaw
against the wind

through burning fields
of savaged oak
through the bones
of a briar patch

you tell your story
at the local fried chicken buffet
without bothering to exhale

oh my gawd,
you say

you just need
some fuel
for the fire.

The Ghosts of Kell Robertson's Chickens

here even the wind
has bones

i can hear you laughing

licking the wounds
of imagination

until nothing
feels invisible
not even death.

Everette Maddox Comes to Belle

we don't have alabama moonlight
or family histories that add up
into anything more than corn whiskey
or biblical floods

our pockets filled with pebbles
and loose change
leave an emotional deficit
no matter how many times
we count them
you say
that's alright
just lay flat
on your back

and look for camelot
as your dreams
cross the mississippi river
floating away
in a brooks brothers suit.

Song of the Dying Possum

there is only one way to look at this

the last thing you see
is the moon dancing
stirring your blood

the last song you hear
is your own.

Poem on Brian Felster's 53rd Birthday

the internet reminds me
that you have been gone now
for nearly 5 years

today we would've eaten bad chinese food
or traded off-color jokes
that now just float around the cosmos
like ping pong balls

while i try to remember
that your dreams
were never anchored
to the earth.

Emilie

it's hard to think of you
in the soil
almost a year

like the sunflowers
you planted
in my uncle's
steel toed work boots

your dancing shoes
turned to dust
scattered into
ome west virginia creek

i used to imagine
that you could move mountains
just by tapping your toes.

Chicken Hungry

like grease clinging
to the carpet
of a marriage

we all need to justify
the price of a buffet.

My First Wife

for lauren snow

when we set up house
in a refrigerator box
on my grandparents'
patio in the suburbs
we never imagined
struggling just to keep
the lights on
with the sun
shining overhead

you picked dandelions
placing them in imaginary flower boxes
just outside our cardboard window
a latch key kid
you taught me
how to kiss
and whistle
through the gap
in my front teeth
as it rained
on our lawn

watering my grandmother's rose bushes

frowning every time
your mother yelled for you

to come in for supper
years later
when i heard
you had gotten
caught up with drugs
like something out of some
lame nancy reagan psa
i wondered if the stuff
you shot in your veins
could ever be as pure
as our love.

Looking for Fathers

for todd moore

it was never so much about bloodlines
as it was about blood.

13 Ways of Looking at a Dying Chinese Town

for d.r. wagner

a one room schoolhouse
on the edge of town

where the ghosts of chinese railroad workers
gave a history to their grandchildren

a boarding house
filled with families
& working girls

where today tourists pick fruit
from low hanging trees
worshipping their roots

cheap wine & baseball on the radio

hit one out of the park
for a paper son

where hamburgers in al the wop's bar
is a thing of beauty

wisdom hangs like a dragon lantern
snapping a rooster's neck
in a display of dominance

the sky is bleeding red
with the fire of ancient songs

& somewhere
off in the distance
your bones are showing.

Poem For Kate Marino

i never saw you drown
your sorrows in swan lake
just stumble home
bouncing from guy to guy
without ever realizing
how much your smile was worth.

Poem For Steven Miller & Brandt Dykstra

we threw parties
where nobody came
but were surrounded by love

where we drank so much
that we told time in empty pitchers

where thousands of people
made beats based on our dreams

where asian girls & half eaten steak sandwiches
waited in the moonlight until well after last call

where our hearts never ran out of darts
or empty bar stools

& the jukebox
seemed as limitless
as the night sky.

Earl

worked the graveyard shift
doing security for the dorms
at my university
before going
to his second job
just to keep his family
in a one bedroom apartment
with a busted elevator
around the corner
from jefferson hospital

at night he'd do the electric slide
or the hokey pokey
to help pass the time
he always had a kind word
for everyone

calling you guy or chief
as if it were a term of endearment

telling us about following tina turner
on his summer vacation
packing his family into a tiny vw van
as if she were the grateful dead

now, *that's a good lookin' lady,* he'd say
before falling asleep at his crossword
just waiting for another chance
to follow
his dreams.

John Prine Never Wrote a Song About That

the moon grazing
in the sweet grass
out for blaze foley's soul

scott wannberg
writing his name
in the snow

a pair of crows
bone tired
of dreaming.

The Gummy Bear Vortex

the indians once fought here
they could hold their whiskey, you say
but dorothy, when it comes to death
the wind has sticky fingers.

Pete Seeger Sings to the Moonlight

he says, love is protest, why carry
a torch for death?

why count the scars
we keep in silence

attaching their limbs to broken words
in place of a melody?

each death is a different song
waiting for the skin
to be reborn

waiting for the night
to rename itself
with our blood.

Future City, Illinois

just north of cairo
where anyone with $20
and a sad story
can relive
the final days
of mark antony
and cleopatra

after the nile ran dry
and the last bus
had stopped running
to thebes.

Frank O'Hara is Dead

i make lists
you make coffins
out of stars.

Poem for David Greenspan

i wonder if phil ochs hung himself
on the same street you grew up on

i wonder if small children
used his bones
to scratch chalk outlines of sunlight
where there had been
only shadows.

To Kell

may god crush
an empty beer can
over your head
so you can bless it.

Mozart and Bobby Driscoll

played for emperors and lions
of the silver screen
before getting thrown
into mass graves

they never even heard
the train
coming.

Swallowing A Hornet's Nest

when i was 7 or 8 years old
my mother's best friend
swallowed a bee
in a can of mountain dew
gasping for breath
as we rushed
to get her to
the emergency room

now we listen to donald trump
on the nightly news

testing history's gag reflex

immune to the sting

we have learned to swallow
almost anything.

We Are Still the Future

i run my fingers
through my beard
white hairs drape around
the corners like flags
with a few more flecks
of ginsberg's shroud
coming in every day
holy in their innocence

i wear every extra pound
like a merit badge
knowing honor isn't something
you can just pin to your chest
and walk away from

knowing that the bus
no longer stops here

knowing that every man
has been an island
in his own heart
at some point

knowing that we all
must pledge allegiance
to something

whether we remember
the words
or not.

Poem for David Laws

girls loved your elvis sideburns
they didn't even notice death
skimming rhinestones
across the mouth
of the youghiogheny river
as you danced
on a cloud.

At 59

greg talks about wasted years
and miss opportunities

they used to pop up
like the sunrise, he says
sipping a flat beer
on his porch
in the middle of winter
in missouri

in his head
he is a young man
watching the berlin wall go down
on a busted black and white tv
imagining the future
while searching for bones
to place on canvas
in the rubble

he crushes a dead leaf
scattering its ashes
in the snow

summer will be here
before we know it, he says

and the sun
will be blood red
with redemption.

Old School Monsters
(Indigent Press, 2017)

Revenge of the Creature

when i was in high school
i liked to hang out in antique stores
rummaging through faded magazines
with dusty pictures of whit bissell or john agar
who had once been married to shirley temple
i liked to imagine the girl in the picture
was the girl in my heart

reinventing the language of monsters

it's no wonder i never went
to the prom.

The Bride of Frankenstein Goes Country

audra modeled her life
after the bride of frankenstein

at fifteen
she was a feminist woman
and a coal miner's daughter
who stood by her man

while blasting sonic youth
in the suburbs.

House of Wax

as the bodies pile up
i think

it could have been shot
in afghanistan.

Being the Fire
(Tangerine Press, 2016)

The Nosebleed Seats in Heaven

in the 9th grade
my mother forced my younger brother
and i to go to a billy graham crusade
at the old three rivers stadium in pittsburgh
where instead of having us run the bases
around the diamond
he preached love
mixed with bigotry
and more than a teaspoon
of hellfire and brimstone
pleading for the all sinners
to come forward
for a laying of hands
right there across home plate

he threw out his slider
his breaking ball
without ever curving
his lips

he said, *in heaven, there are no bad seats,*
and the foam fingers
always form an olive branch.

there in that decaying monument
to the human spirit
where just a few years later

i would be offered a toothless blowjob
by a 48 yr old methhead
at my first rolling stones concert
billy taught me a thing or two
about swagger before mick or keith
ever got the chance

in heaven you just have to know
how to strut like a little red rooster
that's what he taught me
while laying one hand across
my pimple covered forehead
taking away my sins
with a few choice lyrics
of his own.

The Hills Have Eyes

they are my grandmother's
a young raven haired beauty
they were her father's too
red faced every day at noon
turning the sun into a fist.

The Deer Hunter

in greensburg
every boy dreamt
of getting a hunting license
by the age of 12

talking about pickup trucks
shell casings and what sort of antlers
they wanted to have hanging
on the wall in their parents' basement

pat was legally blind at birth
but wanted to be
the pride of his moose lodge
just like everyone else

turned down flat after an eye exam
he waited until after dark
before going into the closet
to find his father's favorite rifle
and headed out into the woods

after a few hours spent freezing
his ass off
in faded camouflage cut offs
he heard something coming toward him
and fired rapidly into the night

as the sun came up
he struggled to push
a dying cow
across several fields to his house
thinking the whole time
that he had bagged the biggest deer in the county

after his father
was forced to pay
a very angry farmer 800 bucks
he never heard the end of it

when he got engaged years later
someone said, *why buy the cow,*
when you can get the milk for free?
he just winced

saying that even milk
ran down his lips
like blood.

The Last Night at Teatro

11-18-95

annie richardson strummed a blue guitar in the doorway
and i worked feverishly on another bad poem
that would never open her heart
and david laws rapped about philosophy
with catholic schoolgirls
who thought he was the second coming
of something less holy
than their crucifix
and genny made jewelry
out of chicken bones
before going to her job at the mall
and steve talked about politics in ireland
and gay chris made everyone smile
and henry and bud thought about better days
and dan talked to linda
about going to high school with jerry garcia
and remembered exactly why he had opened this place
and frank sang hey jude in spanish
and chad joined in on air guitar
and clowney lived up to his name
and adam and marty talked about going on tour
and molly and sarah ann sang silent night
with snowflakes pressed to their tongues
and we all had a moment of silence
for a world that would cease to exist
the second we went out that door.

Making Weight

for steve burrik, 1976-2011

i'm guessing that
you never imagined
being middle aged
at seventeen

steve, in junior high
i wanted to be you
with your shiny doc martens
cheerleader girlfriends
and brand new skateboards
every other week

i didn't realize then
that all glittered
truly wasn't gold

that your father
would knock you around
if you didn't make weight
for the state wrestling championship

or that drugs were more
of a parachute
wrapped around your neck
than they were an escape

after you joined the military
they called you a hero
but it was that scared kid
that i cried for
the night i heard
you'd passed away

when your time came
you went out
eaten up by death

in the end

you were always
just trying
to make weight.

Being the Fire

when i imagined middle age at 23
i never thought about the streets of philadelphia
swept clean of the bones of homeless patriots
i never thought that jumping into the fire
would become no more dangerous than hopscotch

i never thought the pigeons
hovering around rittenhouse square
might one day question my sanity
or that i'd sometimes wish that i could join them
in some unlimited version of our human sky

i never thought that i'd never find love again
or that lloyd would lose his toes to the frost
before diabetes could finish them off
like the vicious shark attack that it is

i was that young
young enough to still fear tornados at bedtime
or a strong kansas wind flying overhead
pony express straight from the emerald kingdom

i never imagined jumping into the fabric of manmade
shadows or having to catch my breath with a butterfly net
that didn't smell of dewar's

i never imagined that time would bless the night
with a rosary of thin skinned dreams
or that i'd have to build a fire on the inside
that was worth jumping into.

Huck's River, Philadelphia

i used to watch as tyrone
hustled every inch of the pavement
between the latimer deli and mcglinchey's bar
strutting as if he ruled the sidewalk
like the conquerors of old

on the streets since just after his 18th birthday
because he lacked the proper identification needed
to click his heels back to some kansas corn field
that his family had settled in
as he put it, *just after the shackles*
had come off of history.

the closest he ever got now
was watching as the barley and hops
floated around the top
of his flat 40oz. hurricane
like mark twain's corpse
searching for a beacon on the delta

as i handed him
a crumpled dollar bill
he told me-

this was huck's river

he was just trying
not to drown in it.

Singh's Song

singh had been called a hindu
an arab
a towelhead
a terrorist
decades before the twin towers
ever quivered
and collapsed
onto the pavement
and into the pages
of history

he had been born
in the streets
of fresno
driving a cab
almost before he could walk

a sikh
he followed a guru
to center city philadelphia
in search of true human equality

while the rest of the world
followed ronald reagan
through death valley days
and beyond

he would walk into dirty frank's
on the corner of pine st.
and start singing
after a single beer
as the patrons groaned
and threatened to fight him
on the sidewalk outside
at three in the afternoon

he would plead
with the bartender
to just let him stay
for one more song
on the jukebox

and somehow sarah
came out cheryl i love you
after someone had left
a weathered cheryl teigs calendar
on the backseat of his jitney in 1987
as his face filled with tears
because he knew
equally was too much
to ask for on a sunny day
in a world
where happy hour
rarely comes
for anyone.

Philadelphia Gentrification Poem

the top floor of my favorite chinese restaurant
got turned into a meth lab.

Children of the Cornbread

for kevin o'neill

one of the last times
i ever saw you
you were getting a hummer
in a parked car on broad street
in the middle of the afternoon

you waved me over
in between moans
and grunts
and bites of fried rice
which you ate with chopsticks
while straddled against the parking brake
of a rusted out '76 eldorado
offering me an egg roll
leaving the napkins
for your date
to wipe her mouth
with.

Y2K: A Love Story

for christina

looking for a small red haired girl
in times square
i remember thinking
there are worse ways
for the world to end.

212 Hours

that's how long i had been awake
when i wrote you that letter
fueled by green tea
from the gas station
across the street
stale cigarettes
coffee from the griffin
and bottom shelf bourbon
from the gay owned and operated diner
on the corner
i wrote three bad drafts
of a paper on kubrick's *2001: a space odyssey*
before i could return to the earth's atmosphere
and tell you i loved you

that was nothing

it took years
before i stopped seeing your skin
in the reflection
of dying stars.

Channeling Bill Bixby

for brendan bailor

fred took me for beers
at the cheap art cafe
around the same time
my father woke up
in the middle of night
clutching his chest
like a re-imagining
of dr. banner's monster

silent for more than 20 years
he had forgotten how to scream
so i did it for him
roaring like a circus lion
as i stumbled back to my dorm room
to survey the damage.

a few years after
my father survived
fred got word
that his younger brother
had been found dead in his apartment
barely old enough to lift a pint

i wasn't there to help him
chase away monsters
one bottle at a time

so i did the only thing
i knew how to
screaming into the night
hoping my voice
would cause stars to tumble
like rocks
lighting his path
as he waited
for the bagpipes
to kick in.

The Treasure of Sam Ryan

there were no femme fatales
on pine street
the day you died

a good catholic boy
fried chicken was your altar
and your cross

john huston never cried
the way you did
over lost loves

you said some things were holy
others were sacred
and that finding religion
was the ability
to tell the difference.

1228 Spruce Street

one side of the street
smelled like fresh laundry
the other was paved
with dandelions
and collection notices.

Sam Ryan Goes to Hollywood

you went there once
with eyes like faded postcards
expecting aspiring starlets
and aging producers
would want to hear
about your grandfather's
journey to america

sam, you once laughed so hard
the dirt fell loose
from under three generations
of fingernails.

The War on Terror and Baklava

the owner of the greek restaurant in town
buys lamb from new zealand every tuesday
he says that paris was just a soft target
that that sort of thing would never fly in st. louis
or ferguson where they teach you how to fight
in the streets.

Dog Shit and Moonlight

we have run out of rabbits
i pull jesus out of my hat
wild dogs scatter by the river.

Ballad of the One Eyed Beast

for greg edmondson

your heart is a highway
made of chicken wire.

Indian Summer in December

murphy chases a stick
the dead chase their shadow
wearing the skull
of a decaying armadillo.

Appalachian Homage to Cid Corman

zen either comes
from the bones
of our fathers

or gets buried
with them.

20 Miles from *Winter's Bone*

the cameras have gone
winter has set in
leaving the spirits
in the wind
to bury
themselves.

Poet Laureate of the Dancing Rabbit

for aaron fine

i imagine hippie girls
taking bacteria showers
making love to strangers
after digging up root vegetables
all morning in the summer sun

i have on clean underwear
and matching socks
and write poems
that aren't comfortable in tents

yesir
i'm happy where i am.

Belle, Missouri: A Book of Hours

for jeanette powers

here we illuminate everything
and find religion
in the treetops
of poems
or barking dogs
who give their song
back to the river
tails wagging.

The Dinner Belle Always Rings Twice

at the dinner belle
young girls in hoodies
fold paper napkins
and shine tarnished butter knives
while whole families
share a single hamburger
and talk about the weather in owensville
this is the only whistle-stop cafe in town
minus the whistle
and the train
going nowhere fast.

Our Friend in Belle

nobody in town
even has a mailbox
and the bus
would stop
running at 2 pm
if only there was one

i'm not sure
i was ever here
the only way to tell
is to read
this poem.

The Village People of Belle

dead indians wrestle
in the treeline
even the moon
is on meth.

Gasconade River Song

the only thing
that keeps me here
is the thought
that a mile
on uneven gravel
is too far to go
for a final baptism.

Gasconade River Song #2

i imagine stars fall from the sky here
like anywhere else
and that flowers take their roots
from the bones
of winter.

Gasconade River Song #3

one day they will place dirt
and stones over my dead body
dropped into some pine box
and weighed down with loose change
and all of the pebbles
from wishing wells.

Gasconade River Song #4

this river makes you think
of all of the lovers
you will never have.

Gasconade River Song #5

a propane tank
lashed against a retaining wall
whines to be set free
as forty feet of water
that started out as sweat
on the forehead of the river
feeds the thirst
of hungry ghosts.

Gasconade River Song #6

as i try to remember
what mick jagger said
about wild horses
an 18 yr old mare
slumps over in a pasture
flooded with waves
of history.

Gasconade River Song #7

mark and tony come from an irish wake
only to discover that the highway
has been closed off
for nearly 300 miles
and that the river
has no respect
for the living
or the dead.

Gasconade River Song #8

she says, *poems about rivers*
are rarely about rivers.

Gasconade River Song #9

heather yells about gender bias
the river sticks out its tongue.

Gasconade River Song #10

here children are raised
to pump gas
to burn their shadows
in effigy

the river only
teaches you
to sing them
to sleep.

Coming of Age River

nobody notices
your voice changing
your sweaty palms
or the flowers blooming
around your mouth.

No Women

there are no attractive women in town
who haven't read the bible
from front to back
like the latest dan brown opus

there are no unattractive ones either

that's okay
i'm still catching up
on dr. suess.

Detroit Poem

a car on fire
in the middle
of the afternoon

this city
is a cannon
shot out
of a cannon.

Poem for Greg Peters

i always wanted to write a poem
that i could leave under your boot soles
like newsprint on a cold february morning
in toledo on the corner of ashland ave
or collingwood blvd. or the sidewalk
outside the cherry street mission

i always wanted to say
that you made the streets feel safer
with your poems
with your laughter
somehow just being
around the corner

i can still hear you
from miles away
my ear pressed
against the pavement
in another city
where time refuses
your body's resignation
to the wind

you say, "our hearts are not
forgotten alleys,
our dreams are only looking
for a place to rest."

Poem for Craig Cody

we shared a motel room
for the better part of 2 months
at 42 you operated the locomotive
at an amusement park
working alongside kids
who weren't even alive
the year you took
your first drink

on your day off
we'd catch a cab
to the local shopping mall
and start downing margaritas
around 10 am

by noon
it was 1975
all over again
you were a new man
with hopes and dreams
and a daughter
who still waited
by the phone
for you to call
while coloring
to the scooby doo theme song

you'd talk about how
you just had to get
down to florida
one last time
as if we were joe buck and ratso rizzo
just trying to make it through
one more winter on the streets

after i left
i heard you wouldn't let the new guy
crash in my bunk
preferring to drink alone
and that when they took you
to the hospital with dts
sunshine was the last thing
you saw from the window
dreaming that you had made it
home
at last.

Eric

worked part time as a driver
for his older sister's escort service
and played guitar on the weekends
smoking weed sunup to sundown
once offering me the pipe

that's when he told me
that he had switched to crack
just for inspiration's sake
and i motioned him away

but when our friend patrice got hooked
it was eric who saved her
from a near pistol whipping
from the biggest coke dealer in the city

eric who told me about how
he had to toss his girlfriend around the room
once smacking her head into a cast iron radiator
just to get off

eric who may or not
have raped a young painter
on the second floor
causing her to run off
like a frightened animal
in the middle of the night

eric who choked his best friend unconscious
in the front parking lot on a sunny afternoon
before heading back in
to listen to curtis mayfield
and breathe in
what was left
of his dreams.

Patrice

once told terry
i'm serving it up on a silver platter,
you're just not coming to dinner.

dead by the age of thirty
her heart exploded on the inside
like a malfunctioning volcano
at an 8th grade science fair
leaving behind three small children
by as many fathers
the daughter of a millionaire
whose money didn't help
her sleep at night
an artist turned crackwhore
she said that picking
the perfect rock
was like shopping for produce
and that sucking cock
could be an art too.

Pam

once told me i was sexier than jesus
but then everyone looks better
when you're microwaving
a frozen burrito
at 3:30 in the morning

that was before she started sleeping
with the building's resident heroin dealer

that was before the fights
and the restless nights
at the cherry street mission

once she invited me into her room
covered with porno tapes from the 1970's
for a sex toy party on her birthday

i told her i had to run out
and that just because i was smart enough
not to step in a puddle
during a lightning storm
that didn't mean
that i could walk on water.

Bianca

bianca's parents owned a dairy queen
and would send her money
that she would use to travel the world
and get blackout drunk
trying to forget
that in high school
she was the spitting image
of fatty arbuckle
in his prime

she would dance in an invisible gymnasium
the ghost of a prom she never went to
going home with anyone who asked
every morning was a clean slate

on new year's she fell headfirst
into an empty organ pit
wearing a concussion
like a crushed paper orchid
pinned against her skull
yelling for someone
to turn up the music
a few hours after
the lights
had gone out.

Brian

when alex and i took the elevator upstairs
to meet brian for lunch
he would only peek his head
out the door

naked as a jaybird
he told us he was covered
head to toe in lube

all 400 plus pounds
of kindness.

Alex

was proof that it took all kinds
a child of privilege
he slept in the back
of a lincoln town car
in the middle of february

when he moved back in
he put electric blankets
on his windows
and warmed his hands
over a george foreman grill

he stole summer sausages
from department stores
to keep meat on his bones
before getting a job
as a bar bouncer

then he met a mexican girl
on a dating website
for the mentally ill

and left toledo forever
to live the american dream
hidden between the pages
of all of the dusty books
floating at the bottom
of lake erie.

Debbie

i remember stumbling out of the coffee shop
the night you got thrown up
against a cop car
for refusing to pay $2
to attend a poetry slam

how you could turn any conversation
into a burning building
your love was so powerful
it could become an accusation
at the drop of a hat

your words lit up the night
like fireflies dipped in battery acid
setting fire to metaphors
in the rain.

Darcie

anyone can live
on the side of a mountain
at the age of 25
it's what you do
when you come down
the other side
that defines you.

Glass City Mantra

you can't eat fame
but failure
can swallow
you whole.

Jessica Keeps a Rotten Watermelon

in the back of her car
for months

the bridge up ahead
is out

drunk
we decide to jump it

pieces of festering melon
fly everywhere

after all these years
the memory of its scent
still seems
like perfume.

Poem for Cherie

as you read poems
about teaching
in the inner city

i think about
what might have happened
if we had met sooner.

Smells like Teen Moms: A Poem for the Lucky Club

for jacob johanson

there is no room service
and the pool is always closed
this is the kind of place
kurt cobain would've stayed in

right before he killed himself.

Poem for Dan O'Neill

we sit on your mother's porch
you strum a banjo
held together with bones
fishing wire
and the blood of celtic warriors
long before your time
but as close as a story away

here it's a wild west show
cole younger
frank james
the mitchell brothers
r.crumb
odd bodkins
the sun rises through the clouds
here it's about myth
and the tales we leave in the dust.

At the Model T Casino

dust shimmers across
the night sky
my heart races
like a beacon
a lonely jackrabbit
in the minimum wage dream factory
the stars have become.

Ryberg's Castle

you sweep dead stars
from the pavement on 39th street
the sun has become a boilermaker
in the middle of the afternoon
your words don't know
east from west
your laughter is dry
and the black coffee
you brew is piping hot
and the poems you write
rise like steam
through the clouds.

Poem for Trixie

your vagina
was a signed
limited edition.

The Russian Sonny and Cher

for s.a. griffin

croon at a wedding on sunset blvd
the minister is passed out in the bathroom
on expensive french vodka
and jerry stahl may well be
the only sober person
in the room.

Poem for Crawdad Nelson

you talk about fort bragg
and edible mushrooms
the folk hero of murder city
the streets of your youth
now flooded over with memories
and bong water.

Cow Shit, Texas

just past 5 am
we cross the new mexico border
and get out of the car
to stretch our legs

a lonesome train whistles
and i think about
a 5th grade history class
that reminded us
to remember the alamo

poor dead davy crockett
is nowhere in sight
and even if he was
he would probably be
passed out drunk
at this hour

across the highway
big vern's steakhouse
advertises the best cut of beef in town
it doesn't matter that it isn't true
my nostrils burn
with the sweet smell of death
and my eyes water
like the rio grande
because even the wind
tastes like a cow pie right now.

Your Last Cerveza

for tony moffeit

a month after todd's death
you're still as pale as a sheet
you meekly offer me
your last cerveza
like a horse thief
who has given up the ghost
now sentenced to travel the prairie
on foot.

Poem for Kell Robertson

you once drew me a map
to the heart of the american southwest
you said, *if you've gone past the barking dogs,*
you've gone too far.

Todd

i'm not sure you ever even held a gun
knives were your thing
but you always used your tongue
to slice words
right down
the middle.

Irina

was born in chernobyl
in the early 1980's
i ask, *what was that like?*

she can't remember her birth
only the beautiful sunset
moments after she exploded
out of the womb.

The Fight Club House

for ryan

had nothing on our place
on w. 23rd street
at least they didn't have to
get up every morning
to pour water into the toilet tank
and they had countless followers
to cut the grass
or shovel the snow
in the middle of january
and there was no mallrat kid
with my signature tattooed
on his ass.

Ryan

ryan and i play darts
in some hick bar
in the middle of mormon country
where everyone is missing
at least one tooth
with a jukebox
that won't play
the song you danced to
the night you lost
your virginity.

Rock of Love

for jason hardung

juice sits on the edge of his couch
down to its last cushion
waiting to see who brett's rock of love is
one of the greatest poets in america
but he can only dream
of power ballads.

Happy Hour at the Gold Coin Saloon

for james ryan morris

young beatniks used to drink here
now they bury their berets
in the woods.

Rocky Mountain High

the local bar has a signed photo
of connie chung on the wall
right next to the men's room

and the vultures
pick at slot machines

it's no wonder
stan brakhage came here
to die.

Ed

tells me
that the elk here
are locally raised

but i'd still rather eat
my shoe.

Tripping at the Olive Garden

luke hands me a brownie
laced with acid
laughing as i run around
a velvet rope
in a strip mall
in the middle
of the afternoon

within minutes
the loch ness monster
swallows jimi hendrix
and approaches my soup bowl.

Jane Fonda Never Said Hello

just left me wondering
if she still saw vietnam
in god's country.

The Dean of the Deli

for dan provost

so much more than your working class roots
a beautiful mind in any alley
you can calculate
what words have cost you
by subtracting the scars
from your heart.

Poem for Jeff Cannon

you said i was a wise man
on a scale of worcester to ten
maybe neil armstrong
but never charles olson.

Round Corner Tavern Poem

for mikey west

every night they mop
the blood of hipsters
off the floor
along with dried semen
and discarded peanut shells

mikey has come here
to fill me with whiskey
before an evening of poetry
about places like this

right now there is a used condom
on the bathroom floor
that has been there since 1978
that has seen war
first loves
and the sadness of last call
it is still more useful
than your average poem.

Running into Gene Avery in the Park

gene rushes over to say hello
his moves are pure scat
he makes me think
of all of the wonderful
joys in this world

right now
100 thousand poets
may stand tall
for change

but i wouldn't change a damn thing.

Scott Wannberg Waves Goodbye to Sacramento

with more character than miss america

after a final bong hit
he dreams of world peace.

Sandy Thomas Goes to Paris

and immediately finds
a free place to stay
there are no sexual expectations
or corny souvenirs

she's just that cool.

The Ghost of Sacramento Past

for gene bloom

the kitchen is full of stock quotes
and racing forms
there is no christmas turkey
and gene has been up half the night
rolling joints in orderly piles
the way they did it in sing sing
the night we put a man
on the moon.

7 for Jori
(Tangerine Press, 2016)

Author's Note

Jori Lirette was a 7 year old boy from Thibodaux, Louisiana, sixty miles west of New Orleans, who had cerebral palsy and was unable to speak and get around on his own. He was decapitated by his father Jeremiah Wright on August 14, 2011. I have attempted to write one poem for every year of his tragically short life. It's that life I choose to honor and not his death, because as a person with cerebral palsy myself, his story could easily have been my own. We are brothers, without the blood. These words are for him.

Sixty Miles West

of the big easy
there was no one
to speak for you

no one to sing to you

your song
a gurgle

a light hum

rattling the window
just above
the butcher's block. (guillotine)

Your First Words

were silence
doves planted
in your mother's mouth

refusing a melody

building ancient cities
along your lips

your body swaying

not some forgotten temple
turned to ember

but a trembling coastline.

The Terrible Twos

at two
you don't
race around the house

or sound out
your name

but nod at the sun
on the pages
of a children's book

where a palsied lion roars

your mother thinks
that could be
you

smiling.

Three Candles

placed in your palm
your father laughs

as your eyes burn
like a tiki torch
in the heart
of god's
forgotten monsters

the fire is yours.

Middle Age

you count stars
on the inside

like grains of sand
washed away
by the moonlight

imagining an entire universe
just out of your reach.

Your 5th & 6th Symphony

shuffling between doctors
you learn to dance
while sitting still

so quiet

as ghosts spell out
your name

in song.

Swansong

barely human
to watchful eyes

guided by voices
a doll to your mother

a dummy used
to make her feel stupid

your head held high
on the sidewalk
for all to see.

John Dorsey lived for several years in Toledo, Ohio. He is the author of several collections of poetry, including *Teaching the Dead to Sing: The Outlaw's Prayer* (Rose of Sharon Press, 2006), *Sodomy is a City in New Jersey* (American Mettle Books, 2010), *Tombstone Factory*, (Epic Rites Press, 2013), *Appalachian Frankenstein* (GTK Press, 2015) *Being the Fire* (Tangerine Press, 2016) and *Shoot the Messenger* (Red Flag Press, 2017) and *Your Daughter's Country* (Blue Horse Press, 2019). His work has been nominated for the Pushcart Prize, Best of the Net, and the Stanley Hanks Memorial Poetry Prize. He was the winner of the 2019 Terri Award given out at the Poetry Rendezvous. He is the former Poet Laureate of Belle, Missouri. He may be reached at archerevans@yahoo.com.

This project was made possible, in part, by generous support from the Osage Arts Community.

Osage Arts Community provides temporary time, space and support for the creation of new artistic works in a retreat format, serving creative people of all kinds — visual artists, composers, poets, fiction and nonfiction writers. Located on a 152-acre farm in an isolated rural mountainside setting in Central Missouri and bordered by ¾ of a mile of the Gasconade River, OAC provides residencies to those working alone, as well as welcoming collaborative teams, offering living space and workspace in a country environment to emerging and mid-career artists. For more information, visit us at www.osageac.org

Osage Arts Community

CPSIA information can be obtained
at www.ICGtesting.com
Printed in the USA
FSHW010710120321
79365FS